Patricia Vadasy

Susan Wayne

Rollanda O'Connor

Joseph Jenkins

Kathleen Pool

Mary Firebaugh

Julia Peyton

A Tutoring

Program in

Phonics-Based

Early Reading

IMPLEMENTATION MANUAL

 SOPRIS WEST EDUCATIONAL SERVICES
A CAMBIUM LEARNING COMPANY

BOSTON, MA • NEW YORK, NY • LONGMONT, CO

ISBN 1-59318-210-4

09 08 07 06   7 6 5

Printed in the United States of America

Published and Distributed by

Sopris West™
EDUCATIONAL SERVICES

A Cambium Learning™ Company

4093 Specialty Place • Longmont, Colorado 80504
(303) 651-2829 • www.sopriswest.com

250IMPMAN/3-06

Dedication

With love to struggling beginning readers and their infinitely patient and talented paraprofessional tutors.

Acknowledgments

We accumulated an extended debt of gratitude over the decade that we designed, field-tested, revised, and evaluated *Sound Partners*. Many individuals and agencies made important contributions to these lessons. The development and research on *Sound Partners* was supported by a series of grants from the U.S. Department of Education, Office of Special Education Programs, and a grant from the Paul Allen Charitable Foundation. Without the support provided by these grants, the development of *Sound Partners* would not have been possible.

Sound Partners is one translation of the rich research base on beginning reading development and instruction. We are indebted to the researchers who built the strong foundation on which applied researchers like ourselves can confidently develop effective applications for practitioners.

Staff and consultants who have contributed to the research and development of the program include: Robert Abbott, Roslyn Adams, Tove Andvik, Lynn Barnicle, Pieter Drummond, Carolyn Hahne, Sally Hurley, Norris Phillips, Scott Stage, Kris Van Valkenberg, and Lynn Youngblood. Many tutors provided immensely valuable feedback and suggestions, including Beverly DeCook, Rayma Haas, Robin Horton, Jeri Lee, Sandy Humphries, Kit Owen, Katia Roberts, Linda Romanelli, Helene Romero, and Janet Stoeve.

The principals and staff (including each building's school secretary who assisted in scheduling, testing, and obtaining parent consents) of our Seattle School District sites made it possible for us to conduct our research and intervention in their buildings. Special thanks go to Cathy Profilet-Shibayama, principal, Viewlands Elementary; Val Wells, Powerful Schools Tutor Coordinator; Greg Tuke, Powerful Schools Executive Director; Susan McCloskey, principal, B.F. Day Elementary; Eric Nelson, principal, Sanislo Elementary; Margo Siegenthaler, Tutor Coordinator, B.F. Day Elementary; and Nancy Chin, principal, Laurelhurst Elementary. We also thank the many teachers in our sites who allowed us to work with the students in their classrooms.

We wish to express our gratitude to Christine Cox, Mary Gallien, and Karla Haden for the typing, design, and preparation of many experimental versions of the lessons.

Finally, we thank all those not named here who assisted us in our work.

Contents

Introduction

Before young children begin to read books, they develop an understanding of the parts of words—the individual sounds or phonemes. Children learn that words are made up of sounds that can be put together in different ways, and that these sounds correspond to the letters in the alphabet. Many researchers have studied how these discrete skills—taking words apart into their individual sounds, blending sounds to make words, spelling words, rhyming, recognizing letter patterns—contribute to reading. Very young children learn these skills by being read to, looking at books with parents, following along with the words, and playing with words that rhyme or start with the same sound.

Phonological awareness is the understanding that words are made up of sounds, or phonemes, that can be manipulated. It includes rhyming, counting syllables, and segmenting spoken words into sounds. Before they can read books, children demonstrate levels of phonological awareness. At an early level, children recognize words that rhyme and words that begin with the same letter sounds. At later levels, children can segment a word into its individual phonemes, blend sounds together to make a word, and discriminate the ending and middle sounds of words. The research is clear that children must have phonological processing skills in order to learn to read. These skills enable the child to understand that words are made up of individual sounds, or phonemes, and that these sounds match with letters of the alphabet.

Phonics describes the relationship between letter sounds and written letters. Because English is a complex language, it can be difficult for children to detect the ways the 44 sounds in our language map onto the 26 letters of the alphabet. Research supports the value of direct instruction in phonics and the regularities of the English language and also shows that training in the skills of segmenting, blending, and letter-sound knowledge, along with opportunities to apply these skills in well-chosen storybooks, has a positive effect on reading acquisition.

This research into the value of phonics is so strong and so clear that we set out to make it possible for nonprofessional tutors—paraprofessional staff, as well as caring parents and adults in the school community—to teach these skills to first graders at high risk for reading problems. *Sound Partners* is a way to provide individual instruction in essential early reading skills to those children who need it most. It offers what many reading experts today advocate: a comprehensive and balanced approach to instruction, including instruction in isolated decoding skills as well as meaning-based learning through increasing amounts of storybook reading.

Sound Partners is designed for tutors who are helping first graders or other students who cannot yet decode. Children who experience difficulty with letter-sound and decoding skills need help learning these skills as quickly as possible so that they can keep up with classmates and take advantage of classroom reading instruction. We know that children who are doing poorly in reading at the end of first grade are likely to remain poor readers. It is very difficult to correct reading problems, and children with reading problems are likely to fall farther and farther behind their classmates. Intensive early intervention in the form of individual tutoring is one effective way to prevent reading failure.

This Implementation Manual is written for the person who supervises the *Sound Partners* program at each school site. The manual describes the instructional components of *Sound Partners*, because the supervisor must be able to assist tutors to use the lessons. It also summarizes the research base and discusses issues to consider when organizing a *Sound Partners* program.

Research Base of *Sound Partners*

Sound Partners was extensively field-tested from 1993–2002 under a series of research grants from the U.S. Department of Education. During that time, the program was implemented in typical urban public school settings, in buildings serving large numbers of students from low-income, minority, and limited-English-speaking backgrounds. In most of our research, the tutors were either paraprofessionals or instructional assistants already working in the schools. All research targeted first-grade students, although the program has also been used for older students.

From 1993–1997, we pilot-tested *Sound Partners* in four urban elementary schools in a series of four experimental studies, comparing tutored students to nontutored peers. Since 1998, we have tested several versions of *Sound Partners* in more than a dozen urban elementary schools in four quasi-experimental studies to identify the instructional components that are most effective when used by paraprofessional tutors. These studies have been published in peer-reviewed journals, cited in the Bibliography.

One widely used indicator of program effectiveness is student performance on standardized (adjusted for age) reading measures. The students in our studies were assessed on word attack, word identification, and spelling measures. Mean, overall, pretest reading and spelling scores (at the beginning of first grade) for the students in our studies averaged 80.2, equivalent to the bottom 10th percentile. After approximately 40 hours of tutoring (or 80 tutoring sessions), students averaged 100.5 on posttest at the end of first grade, equivalent to the 50th percentile.

Another widely used indicator of program effectiveness is the effect-size statistic, which is the difference between the mean scores of *Sound Partners* students and those of nontutored controls, expressed in terms of standard deviation units. Effect sizes for *Sound Partners* have ranged from small to quite large, averaging $d = .70$ across all years (1993–2002).

The Supervisor's Role

Your role as supervisor is to oversee *Sound Partners* implementation in the school. In order to do this effectively, you should know the program very well and be familiar with the procedures for implementing each part of the lessons in order to model for tutors and to correct their errors. *Sound Partners* is most successful when the supervisor is a special education, Title I, or reading teacher with a background in early reading instruction.

Head tutors or tutor coordinators can also be effective supervisors, especially if they have had substantial experience using *Sound Partners*.

To ensure that *Sound Partners* tutoring is as effective as possible, the supervisor:

- ▶ Assists with placement of students who need to start at a higher level than Lesson 1.

- ▶ Monitors tutor attendance.

- ▶ Becomes familiar with each tutor and student.

- ▶ Monitors that the space allocated for tutoring is suitable. If the tutoring space is too noisy or is needed by other school staff, arrange for alternative space.

- ▶ Checks tutor implementation once a week (using the Tutor Observation Form) and note tutor delivery of lessons; provides feedback if needed.

- ▶ Administers and/or reviews students' mastery tests, and adjust student placement in lessons as needed.

- ▶ Makes tutors feel comfortable asking for assistance when needed.

- ▶ Suggests alternative strategies when students have difficulty learning a skill.

- ▶ Advises additional review for a student who needs more practice on skills before moving on.

- ▶ Advises that a student who finds the lessons too easy and unchallenging be moved up and allowed to skip some lessons.

- ▶ Arranges follow-up in-service training or consultation for tutors.

- ▶ Oversees tutor hours and payroll.

Selecting Students

Sound Partners is designed to serve students entering first grade who lack essential early reading skills. These are children who may not be able to rhyme, do not know most of their letter sounds, are not able to blend letter sounds together to sound out words, and cannot segment words into phonemes. In the large urban school district where we field-tested lessons, we selected students from the bottom 20% of first graders tested on these skills. Methods of selection for tutoring vary, depending upon a school's resources. We suggest that schools use a combination of the following methods.

Kindergarten Teacher Assessments
For first grade students who attended kindergarten in the same school, it is usually possible to obtain the kindergarten teacher's assessment of the students' early reading skills. Often, kindergarten teachers can predict which students will need extra reading help in first grade.

First Grade Teacher Prediction

We asked first grade teachers (after the third week of school) which children they believed would not be reading at grade level at the end of the year. We then assessed those children more carefully.

Title I and Special Education Teacher Assessment

Within the first few weeks of school the special services staff often identify first graders who will need extra reading assistance.

Title I Testing Procedures

Some schools will be able to use their methods for identifying first graders for Title I reading assistance to choose students for tutoring. These tests often include letter recognition/naming, detecting beginning and ending consonant sounds, sound substitution, and sight-word recognition.

In our research we have found that letter-naming rate and phoneme-segmenting skill ability are good first grade (and kindergarten) predictors of reading outcomes.

Recruiting and Selecting Tutors

The key to a successful and smoothly operating *Sound Partners* program is good tutors. These are individuals who know the importance of learning to read, who understand the need to follow lesson instructions, who enjoy working with young children, and who are dependable. We have found that there are individuals like these in all communities.

Recruiting Tutors

There are several ways to find good tutors:

▶ **Paraprofessionals**—Paraprofessionals or instructional assistants already employed in the school are very effective *Sound Partners* tutors. They may be trained to use *Sound Partners* for all or part of their work with individual students.

▶ **School Newsletter**—Many schools successfully recruit parent tutors with an announcement in the school newsletter at the beginning of the year. Parents can be dedicated and reliable tutors. Although parents should not tutor their own child, parent tutors recruited from the same school as their children care strongly about the success of the other children in the school. We recommend that schools target recruitment at parents of children in kindergarten and first grade, as these are the parents who are most likely to tutor for more than one year.

▶ **High School Counselors**—Schools have tried to use high-school-age tutors in our program. We find that high school students can make excellent tutors but often need *much* more supervision. These young tutors often come without previous work skills and may need to be taught basic job behaviors such as being on time, coming every day, and managing young children. High school counselors are able to identify students who need or are interested in community service, or who are considering careers in teaching.

These students, under *much* careful supervision, can be effective *Sound Partners* tutors.

▶ **Retired Individuals**—Many retired persons would like to continue their involvement in their community, and tutoring young children often satisfies that interest. They can be recruited through announcements in church bulletins or retirement communities.

Selecting Tutors

Once you have a pool of tutor applicants, selection procedures should always include:

▶ A state police check on their history of criminal violations (follow district fingerprinting requirements).

▶ A check of their ability to read and speak English, as they will need to follow written instructions and model letter sounds correctly.

Basic Instruction Guidelines

Students will start out in the *Sound Partners* program at different points, and some will have more reading skills than others. The tutor's goal is to accelerate each student as fast as possible, while also making sure that the student masters all the skills in the lessons before going on. To help tutors pace their instruction and review, there are review cycles built into the lessons for those students who need additional practice. The lessons are designed so that when tutors follow them closely, the student will be working on skills that are not yet mastered and reinforcing previously taught skills through varied practice and repetition.

Based on our work since 1993 training tutors and studying the *Sound Partners* program, we have identified tutoring requirements that are critical for student success in learning early reading skills. *Sound Partners* is effective when tutors:

▶ Follow the lessons and don't improvise or leave out parts of the lessons.

▶ Use a brisk pace and are organized, so that students are engaged and their learning time is maximized.

▶ Get to know their students' skills and needs by carefully observing them and learning their strengths, weaknesses, and areas of growth.

▶ Tutor consistently four or five days per week.

▶ Provide specific praise.

Sound Partners differs from many tutoring programs in its structure and tutor expectations. The lessons clearly lay out the sequence of skills and practice activities that tutors will present. While the instructional sequence is prescribed, the tutor does individualize the lessons for each student. The tutor does this by carefully observing each student's progress and mastery of skills, and by providing the appropriate level of support and review. The

tutor scaffolds the level of assistance he provides to the student and adds more practice where it is needed.

Sound Partners Lesson Features

The *Sound Partners* lessons contain common, basic components that change gradually so that lessons proceed in a very predictable fashion for the tutors and their students. The basic components are described in detail in this section.

Early lessons (1–30) cover instruction in most common sounds of individual letters and letter pairs, as well as containing practice in segmenting words into phonemes and a strategy for sounding out unfamiliar words composed of previously taught letter sounds. Spelling practice, word lists, and storybook reading are added throughout the lessons. Irregular or sight words are also taught in the early lessons. In the middle set of lessons (31–60), the phonemic awareness activities are faded out, and more phonics instruction and reading and spelling practice are added, including words with initial/final blends, magic -e- words, and word endings. (e.g., **-s**, **-ed**, **-ing**, and **-y**). Finally, the later lessons (61–100+) continue to teach letter-sound combinations and introduce strategies for reading longer words. Story reading also takes up a bigger part of lesson time. A detailed Scope and Sequence chart that describes the lessons and their components is in the Appendix.

How to Lay Out Lesson Materials
The lesson pages are designed for the tutor to sit on the right side of the student. This allows the tutor to more easily read the tutor text on the right-hand side of the lesson pages, and the student can more easily read the large print on the left-hand side of each lesson page. *Sound Partners* lessons are laid out in a consistent pattern so that the tutor and student can sit side by side and easily read and work from their respective parts of the lesson pages.

Boxes Around Letters, Pairs, and Words
A box around a letter, letter pair, or word means that a new sound or word is being introduced, and the tutor must first model whatever is in the box. The tutor will say, for example: "This is our new letter, m̲. It makes the sound /m/ like in 'moon.' Now you point to the letter and say the sound." Letter names are underlined, and letter sounds are enclosed by diagonal lines / /.

Tutor Text vs. Student Text
The column of text on the right-hand side of each page includes the tutor directions. This column may contain the directions for a new lesson component, or a reminder for the tutor. This column also contains the tutor's script—what the tutor says to the student to present that particular lesson activity. The tutor script is enclosed with quotation marks. The tutor does not typically need to prepare any added explanation unless the student does not understand the directions or needs vocabulary instruction.

Student Reading Procedures

When the student works on each lesson activity, he or she should read the word lists or letter lists moving from left to right in each row. This will reinforce in the student the left-right orientation of print. The student should always fingerpoint to each item on the lesson page. Fingerpointing increases student accuracy, and it allows the tutor to keep track of which item the student is working on.

Spelling

Whenever the tutor instructions show a pencil icon, the tutor will direct the student to spell by writing. There are opportunities to practice spelling as a written task in the Say the Sounds, Word Reading, Pair Practice, and Sight Word lesson components. The tutor dictates several words for the student to write. After the student writes a word, the tutor always asks the student to read the word aloud. Tutors can individualize the lessons by giving the student more or less spelling practice, as needed. Tutors will usually begin spelling practice with a newly introduced letter sound or word, one that the student finds difficult, and end with a letter or word that the student can be successful with.

Print Conventions

Letter names are underlined (e.g., a) and letter sounds are enclosed by diagonal lines / / (e.g., the letter sound for the letter a is /a/).

Lesson Coverage

Students will move at different rates through *Sound Partners* lessons. All tutors will begin tutoring their students at Lesson 1 on day one of tutoring, but they pick up on day two at many different points in the lessons—some still on Lesson 1, some at the end of Lesson 2. Children participating in our studies completed anywhere from 60 to over 100 lessons by the end of the school year. To ensure that each child makes maximum progress, the tutor must carefully control the pace at which the student works through the lessons. A student who finishes only two lessons in a week may actually make more progress than another who completes four but was merely reviewing material that had already been mastered.

Finding an appropriate pace for each student is not easy, but you can help by showing the tutor how to check the student's level of accuracy in each lesson. If a student's responses are correct 95–100% of the time, the tutor may need to move the student forward in the lessons to more challenging material. If the student's performance on a task like sounding out is still only correct 20% of the time when explicit practice on sounding out is about to be phased out of the lessons, then the tutor will need to go back and review at least that section of the lessons until performance improves. Performance on the mastery tests (which can be given every 10 lessons) is another way to assess whether a student is placed appropriately and which skills need more practice. Student copies of the mastery tests are available in the lessons.

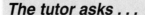

If a student is absent, should I skip the lessons he missed, or repeat previous lessons?

When a student is absent, the tutor should pick up where she left off at the student's last lesson. Often this is where the student should be. If the student has been having difficulty, or has had a long absence, the tutor may need to go back and repeat lessons, starting at the point where the student is about 90% accurate on lesson content.

Individual Lesson Components

On the following pages, we first describe each *Sound Partners* lesson component and then include common questions that tutors have about implementing each component.

Say the Sounds (and First Sounds)

In early lessons, individual sounds are taught both in isolation ("<u>A</u>. What sound does this letter say?") and in the context of a word ("*Apple*. What's the beginning sound in *apple*?"). The student practices the beginning sounds activity with difficult letters to facilitate quick retrieval of sounds. Progress in letter-sound identification is critical to success in the program. Cumulative review of the sounds is built into the lessons. In the second half of the program, the student is introduced to letter combinations, including consonant blends, diphthongs, digraphs, and vowel teams.

It is critical that tutors model correct letter sounds. When training new tutors, you should always model the sound for each letter in the alphabet, as well as the letter pairs. Have trainees take turns going through the alphabet saying letter sounds. Correct trainees when needed. An audiotape on letter sounds can be used for training. Emphasize that tutors will be teaching the *short* vowel sounds. The vowel sounds will be the most difficult sounds for students to learn and discriminate. Students will confuse /a/ and /e/, /e/ and /i/, and /o/ and /u/. Check that trainees model correct vowel sounds.

There are two types of letter sounds: continuous and stop sounds. *Continuous* sounds like /aaa/ and /mmm/ can be stretched out; *stop* sounds like /b/ and /d/ are said quickly. When training, list the stop sounds for tutors (b, d, c, q, t, p, and k). Caution tutors not to add an "uh" sound after b and d. Stop sounds should be spoken quickly without adding a vowel sound at the end.

If students have difficulty remembering letter sounds, tutors should use the word cues that pair each letter sound with a word. If the classroom teacher uses a different key word for each letter, the tutor should use those words. Remind the tutor to be consistent and always use the same word (e.g., /**e**/ as in **E**d). The student uses the word to recall the sound.

When letter pairs are introduced, students have key words to pair with the letters. The student reads the underlined letter pair first, then reads the whole word. The lessons always provide examples of words that include the target letter pair (should the tutor forget what the letter pair sounds like in isolation).

After the student says all the letter sounds, the tutor has the student write the letter for the most recently introduced sound and other sounds that are not yet automatic. When a tutor asks a student to write a letter, the tutor says the letter *sound*, not the letter name ("Now write the letter that says /aaa/.").

Letter Sounds Cards

If a student is not learning letter sounds at the rate the sounds are being introduced and reviewed in the lessons, the tutor should add practice. The tutor can do this by pairing each sound with the key word in the lessons. As noted earlier, if the classroom teacher uses different key words to teach letter sounds, substitute those in the tutoring lessons.

The tutor can also add practice in letter-sound correspondence by using the Letter Sounds Cards. For a few minutes at the beginning of a tutoring session, the tutor can have the student practice a group of letters that are difficult for the student. The student points to each letter or letter pair, going first from letter to sound, then from sound to letter. If the student is having difficulty reading the ea letter pair, the tutor has the student point and say: ea, *leaf*, /ea/ (letter names, key word, and letter sound). If the student was having difficulty spelling the letter pair, the student would point and say: *leaf*, /ea/, ea (key word, letter sound, and letter names).

The tutor asks . . .

When I'm teaching the letters, does it matter if the student tells me the letter name or the letter sound?

The *Sound Partners* program focuses on letter-sound knowledge, which is critical for students learning to read. Many students who already know the names of the letters are not able to match each letter and its sound. Tutors work with their students on the letter sounds in the early lessons. It is very important that tutors know the correct sound for each letter and model this for the student—for example, a quickly sounded /d/ and /p/ for these stop sounds, and not /duh/ and /puh/. It is most important that tutors model the correct short vowel sounds, as many children have difficulty discriminating between the /a/ and /e/ sounds, the /e/ and /i/ sounds, and the /o/ and /u/ sounds.

Segmenting

This activity teaches the student to separate words into individual phonemes. It is an auditory activity, and the student must learn to do it *without* looking at the word. Students learn to segment words into three and four phonemes. This activity can be very difficult for some students, but with repeated practice it can be mastered by all students. Tutors model the skill for the student, and a set of divided boxes is used as a visual cue. It is very important that during this activity the tutor and the student stop between each sound and not blend sounds together as in the Word Reading section. The ability to segment words is particularly useful to children as they begin to write and spell. Tutors should encourage students to first orally segment a word that they have difficulty spelling.

After the tutor says each word, the student should first repeat the word so the tutor knows the student heard it correctly. The task requires the student to point and say one sound for each box. The tutor should correct the student if the sounds overlap (e.g., /m/... *map*), and then model the correct response (/m/ /a/ /p/).

If the student needs assistance with four-phoneme segmenting with consonant blends, sound out the word slowly, say the sounds yourself and have the student point to the boxes. If the student needs more assistance, write the letters above the boxes, then fade out these forms of assistance. Segmenting is an *auditory* (listening) task; the student should not be reading and should not see the words. He should be able to segment just by hearing the word. Cover the printed words if necessary.

The tutor asks . . .

Why is segmenting important?

The segmented boxes provide a concrete means of teaching children how to break words into individual phonemes. It helps make children aware that words are made up of separate sounds. They do this activity as they are also learning that each sound is associated with a letter of the alphabet or with a combination of letters. They build up to separating four-phoneme words that include initial and final consonant blends.

My student has just begun segmenting four-letter words with consonant blends in the sound boxes. Most of the time he can't do it—he can't seem to hear the inside consonant in a word like "sent." Is there anything I can do to help him?

One strategy is for the tutor to tell the student, "I'll say the sounds and you point to the box each sound goes in." After the student is able to do this, the tutor and student switch roles, and the student says the sounds as the tutor points. Finally, the student points to the boxes, then says the sounds and points.

Another strategy that helps some students is for the tutor to write the letters of the word above the box and have the student sound each one out and point to the appropriate box.

Once the student can segment with these aids, the tutor returns to the unassisted segmenting task. Students must learn to segment words without printed letters, just by listening to the words. This skill enables them to spell words correctly.

Word Reading

For many students, learning to sound out words properly is the beginning of independent reading success. Once students master the letter sounds in a given word and can say the stretched-out sounds together quickly, they may master the sounding-out skill in ten or fewer lessons. Some students will have more difficulty identifying letter sounds, holding the sequence of sounds in memory, and running the sounds together so that they recognize the word. These students will need more practice in the sounding-out skill.

The lesson formats describe how to sound out words properly. Being able to sound out words is the most important skill *Sound Partners* tutors teach. Children should not progress to subsequent lessons until they have mastered sounding out. Whenever a student encounters a difficult decodable word in a text, the tutor scaffolds or corrects the student by asking the student to sound it out.

Supervisors should emphasize that sounding out is a very important strategy, and tutors should teach it carefully. Tutors model sounding out *without* stopping between sounds. Move immediately from one sound to the next (e.g., "sssaaammm," *not* /s/-/a/-/m/). Tutors should really exaggerate *stretching* continuous sounds. They should not continue with lessons until the student can demonstrate how to use this strategy. Tutors should not accept recognizing and reading a word by sight as a correct response when they begin to teach the sounding-out skill. The student must demonstrate the strategy in order to be able to decode new words. Sometimes it helps to describe this stretching out of sounds as "singing" or "humming" the sounds.

Sounding-Out Scaffolding

If a student cannot blend a three-phoneme word, like <u>bat</u>, tutors should:

▶ Cover the last letter.

▶ Have the student blend the first two phonemes: "baaa."

▶ Then, have the student add the last phoneme: "baaat."

At the end of Word Reading, students practice spelling words they are learning to read. The tutor dictates, and the student writes the words on a piece of paper or in a notebook. Tutors should choose words the student needs to practice. They should also include words with newly introduced sounds, sounds the student needs to practice, and sounds the student can spell successfully. Students should always reread the words they spell. When the student has difficulty spelling a word, the tutor should encourage the student to segment the word into its sounds and then write the letters that match the sound. Tutors can use large graph paper for this phoneme-to-grapheme mapping.

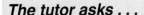

The tutor asks . . .

Is it important that the student not stop between the sounds when sounding out a word?

Sound Partners teaches students to blend the sounds together continuously to help them decode and identify unfamiliar words. If the student stops between the sounds, she will often not be able to hear and recognize the word she is decoding. That said, some students who have already learned in their classrooms to stop between each sound when blending have been able, through tutoring, to make sense of the words they were decoding in that manner. If the student is sounding out words successfully with this strategy, the tutor shouldn't try to teach the student a new strategy that may just confuse the student.

Sight Words

Many words are not phonetically regular or cannot be sounded out with the limited skills early readers have. Some of these words (e.g., "of," "was," "they") occur very frequently in children's books and must be treated differently by the tutor and reader.

In the Sight Words section of the *Sound Partners* lessons, most irregular words are introduced before they are encountered in text. The tutor introduces a new sight word by reading it and then asking the student to read the word, point to each letter, spell the word, and read the word again. While students are not told *not* to sound out these words (how would they know which words are which?), they are taught that some words sound out funny and need to be remembered. In fact, when young readers attempt to sound out irregular words, they often get helpful clues about the word. These phonemic clues, along with memory and context, allow students to read these words. When correcting errors on irregular words, tutors simply provide the correct word for the student and have the student reread it.

If a student has difficulty learning frequently used sight words (e.g., "the," "for," "to," and "said"), the tutor makes flash cards for these words. Tutors explain to the student that these are words we all read lots of times, so it is important to learn to read them quickly and easily.

Reading Long Words

Beginning in Lesson 61, students are introduced to multisyllable words and words with endings, prefixes, and suffixes. First, students practice reading compound words, and later they learn inflected words and words with affixes.

Compound Words

The tutor covers part of the word and lets the student read the uncovered part. Then the tutor does the same with the other part of the word. Next, the tutor asks the student to put the parts together. Later, the student covers part of the word herself.

Multisyllable Words

The tutor first models breaking words into syllables. Then the student practices reading words chunked into syllables. Finally, the student must break words into syllables and then read the whole word.

Magic -e-

Beginning in Lesson 46, students are introduced to the magic -e- rule: If a word has an e on the end, the middle vowel says its name and the e is quiet. First, the student learns to identify the middle letter (the vowel) and the long vowel sounds, and to notice if a word ends in e. Then the student identifies the names of the middle letters in a list of words. Finally, the student practices reading and discriminating words with and without a magic -e- ("cut" and "cute," "nap" and "nape").

The student is taught to identify and read magic -e- words in stages through sequenced instruction with lists of words.

Stage 1

The tutor introduces the rule: "If a word has an e at the end, the middle vowel says its name, and the e is quiet." The tutor helps the student to find the middle letter (vowel) in words and to notice whether a word ends in e. The tutor helps the student to identify the sound of the middle letters.

Stage 2

The tutor asks the student to read mixed lists of words, some with and some without a magic -e-. The tutor corrects the student, if necessary, by reminding the student of the rule.

Although the tutor will often remind the student of the magic -e- rule, students are *not* expected to memorize/say the rule.

Tutors should encourage students to notice magic -e- words in the stories. Tutors should praise students (using *specific* praise) when they notice students correctly reading these words (in context) after students have recently learned the rule.

Word Endings

The lessons introduce common word endings. The tutor teaches an ending by pointing to an isolated word ending (e.g., -ing) and saying words with the ending. *Tutors should not pronounce endings in isolation.* The tutor then has the student look at an ending (e.g., -s) and say a word with the ending. The lessons provide practice in reading words with endings and do not attempt to teach spelling rules. The lessons teach the -s, -ed, -ing, and -y endings, with the goal that students be able to read words with these endings.

Pair Practice

This component (beginning in Lesson 43) provides another format for practicing letter-pair correspondences. There is considerable spell-

ing-sound predictability in English at the letter-pair unit level. The tutor dictates letter-pair sounds for the student to write and has the student read and spell both words and nonwords with letter pairs that have been introduced.

The tutor corrects by asking the student to say the letter-pair sound (for reading) or remember the letters that make the sound (for spelling). The tutor should have the student refer to the Letter Sounds Card, if needed, to retrieve letter-pair information.

Mini-Components

Mini-components that last for two to four lessons provide added phonics instruction. These only appear in certain lessons. A brief description of each mini-component follows.

Final m and n Blends (Lessons 43–46)
The letter sounds /m/ and /n/ are nasal sounds that are produced by air in the nasal cavity. It is difficult to hear these sounds when they occur in a final blend, due to coarticulation. The tutor helps the student become aware of these sounds by contrasting word pairs, one with and one without a final nasal m or n blend.

Inside-Sound Spelling (Lessons 39–42)
Because many phonemes seem to disappear when they are coarticulated in words, the tutor offers the student practice in recognizing these elusive phonemes. The tutor provides the student with contrasting word pairs, one with and one without a consonant blend.

Spelling Similar Sounds (Lessons 49–51)
Students often confuse the spellings for words containing tr and ch because of coarticulation. The /r/ and /ch/ sounds are produced in a similar manner, and when the /t/ and /r/ sounds are coarticulated, the sound is made in the same part of the mouth as the /ch/ phoneme. The tutor provides the student with practice reading and spelling word pairs that contrast the two pairs, which helps the student be more aware of the /r/ in tr blends.

Long u Sounds (Lessons 53–56)
In magic -e- words, the u may either sound like /oo/ as in tune or like /y-u/ as in cute. The student practices identifying which long u sound occurs in words. Students need to try both sounds when they are reading unfamiliar long u words.

Useful Word Chunks (Lessons 57–59)
The tutor teaches the -igh and -ight families because they appear in many of the *Sound Partners* storybooks. The student practices reading and spelling words in these families.

Double Consonants (Lessons 72–74)
The tutor teaches the rule for words with double final consonants: If a single-syllable word with a short vowel ends in f, s, l, or z, the final letter is usually doubled. The student practices spelling single-syllable words (ending in f, s, l, or z) both with and without a short vowel.

Contraction Review (Lessons 95 and 99)

The tutor teaches the student how to determine when and where apostrophes should appear in words. First, the student reads a list of contraction words in different word families. The student then practices the long way of saying each contraction (breaking it up into two words) and identifies the missing letters in each contraction. Finally, the student is given practice in spelling these words.

Book Reading Instructions

After the first 15–20 minutes of hard work on the component reading skills during the first part of the lesson session, students and tutors alike enjoy applying those skills during the storybook reading. If the student has mastered sound identification, sounding out, and word lists, reading the story will be fun and rewarding. The lessons have been designed to require a minimum of instruction during book reading, and the activity affords practice in the component skills. Of course, students will make errors, and error correction is an important part of instruction.

The repeated reading of the storybooks in the lessons builds fluency (rate and accuracy). Students need lots of practice rereading familiar text to build confidence and success. Book reading guidelines—including time spent on reading, which books to read, how to read with the student, how to correct student errors, and two reading rules—are outlined below.

General Guidelines

With many students, tutors will be able to complete all of the lesson components before it's time to read books; this is obviously most desirable. However, book reading is a balancing act. If a student is struggling with the lesson content, she may not cover the entire lesson before it's time to read. In this case, the student may not be able to read independently because she has not yet mastered all of the subskills that are assumed to have been taught prior to book reading.

Advise your tutors that they should do their best to cover as much of the lesson as possible prior to Book Reading. If need be, they can help the student read with echo or partner reading (see below). Tutors should schedule reading time during each 30-minute session, using the method that best matches the student's reading ability.

Some general guidelines:

1. Book Reading is the last activity in *each tutoring session*. If a lesson is not completed and it is time for Book Reading (last 10–15 minutes of the tutoring session), the tutor should have the student reread the book assigned to the most recently *completed* lesson.

> **Example for the tutor:** You are working with your student on the middle portion of Lesson 34, and you have reached the last 10 minutes of the tutoring session. Skip step 1 of the Book-Reading Steps (below), and have the student reread the book assigned to Lesson 33, *The Big Hat*. Then have the student reread other previously read books for the remaining time.

2. Time spent on book reading varies by lesson number. For the first half of the lesson sequence, tutors should spend 10 minutes reading at the end portion of each tutoring session (the second half of the lesson sequence requires 15 minutes of reading).

3. Tutors should try to *complete as many Book-Reading Steps* as possible. If a book has been assigned to multiple consecutive lessons (e.g., the book *Samantha* is assigned to four lessons, 67–70), tutors skip step 2 of the Book Reading Steps, and go from step 1 to step 3.

4. If there is time left over, and the tutor has completed *all* Book-Reading Steps, the tutor begins the next lesson. This is likely to occur only in the early lessons when there are not as many books to read. There are also Supplementary Reading suggestions spaced sporadically throughout the lessons.

Book-Reading Time

Lessons	Minutes
6–49	10 minutes
50–100+	15 minutes

Book-Reading Steps

Step 1:   Tutors and students read the book assigned to the lesson twice, *if it is the first time the book appears in the lessons.* If it is the second, third, or fourth consecutive time the book appears in the lessons, tutors and students read it through once and go to step 3 (e.g., *The Big Hat* is assigned to Lessons 32–33. Read *The Big Hat* twice for Lesson 32 but only once for Lesson 33).

Step 2:   Tutors and students read the previous lesson's book once.

Step 3:   If there is time left, reread previously read books from earlier lessons.

Book-Reading Methods

Method	Definition
Independent	Student reads aloud by him or herself.
Partner	Student and tutor read aloud together.
Echo	Tutor reads one line of text aloud, and then student rereads same line. Repeat process throughout book.

Book-Reading Error Correction

When the student makes a reading error, the tutor isolates the difficult sounds in the word, and helps the student blend the word. If it is a sight word, the tutor simply provides the correct word. The tutor always has the student reread the entire sentence in which the word appears. This is important, so we will repeat it:

▶ The tutor isolates the sounds and directs the student to the difficult portion/sounds in the word, and helps the student sound out and/or blend the word. If the word is a sight word, the tutor simply provides the correct word.

▶ The tutor has the student reread the corrected word and then the entire sentence with the word in context.

Book Reading: Two Rules
Students must follow two rules for storybook reading:

1. *Always* fingerpoint. There is an amazing difference in accuracy and fluency when early readers track each word with their finger when reading. Fingerpointing also lets the tutor follow along. Many children resist this for some reason. Tutors should model by pointing for themselves when they read for their students.

2. *Reread* any sentence with an error, for added practice ("Let's read that again"). Tutors should correct *all* errors immediately by supplying the word (if it is a sight word or if it has not previously been taught) or by having the student sound out the word (when all sounds are known and/or the word has appeared in the lessons). After the student or tutor corrects an error, the student *always* returns to the beginning of the sentence and rereads. This procedure allows smoother reading for comprehension and extra practice on difficult words. Using this procedure consistently and positively helps student progress.

Book-Reading Discussion
Tutors should briefly discuss the book with students before, during, and after reading by asking the following or similar questions:

▶ What do you already know about (book topic)?

▶ What happened so far?

▶ What were the most important ideas?

▶ What do you think will happen next?

▶ Briefly, tell me the story in your own words.

The tutor asks . . .

My student refuses to fingerpoint when he reads.

One way to avoid this argument is for the tutor to make it clear from the start that, "We fingerpoint when we read when we are together." If this has been taught inconsistently, the tutor may be able to get the student to point with the eraser of his pencil. As a last resort, the tutor can fingerpoint for the student, making sure that the student is following along.

If a student reads accurately but very slowly, does it matter?

The ultimate goal of reading instruction is to enable the student to read fluently with comprehension of what she is reading. When a student reads very slowly, word by word, it is difficult for the student to get the meaning of the text, and the student becomes unmotivated to read. Once a student is beginning to blend and decode words accurately, the tutor should encourage the student to read at a pace at which she gets the meaning of the text. The tutor can check this by asking the student a question about the sentence or page the student just read. Then the tutor can coax (but not push or rush) the student to read a little bit faster by saying:

▶ "Now let's try reading the next page really smooth."

▶ "Can you try to read the next page a little bit quicker?"

▶ "Let's try to read this page like you were reading it to your little brother."

Why do children read well one day but not the next?

Many factors may account for a student's variable reading performance during tutoring. A first grader's attentiveness and alertness will influence reading. The tutoring setting may influence the student's desire to perform well on a particular day. If a story contains difficult, new letter sounds or blends that have been recently introduced, accuracy and fluency will decline. Finally, first graders often experience many childhood illnesses, and a student who has been out sick with a virus or chicken pox may take a few weeks to feel completely well again.

How can I encourage my student to read more carefully—so often it seems like he just isn't paying attention or trying?

Fingerpointing is one way to help beginning readers focus on the individual words in a story. If a student is just guessing at the words or making up his own story, tutors should cover the pictures in the story with an index card and ask the student to read without the illustrations. Tutors can use a simple point system to reinforce the student for fingerpointing and for paying attention to the story.

Why does the student have to reread any sentence with an error?

In these lessons, one goal of story reading is to practice the decoding skills that are taught in the rest of the lesson. After the student shows the tutor that he knows the letter sounds and sounding-out strategy, he applies those skills in a story carefully chosen so that he will have to use those skills. If a student comes across a word that he doesn't know, he uses the strategies he has been taught, and if he still doesn't know the word, the tutor provides it. By rereading the sentence, the student gets more practice reading a difficult word and also regains the sense of the sentence. After the student rereads the sentence, the tutor gives specific praise for how much the student improved his speed or accuracy.

Why aren't there more comprehension activities in the program?

Sound Partners is carefully designed to teach the lowest 20% of first graders a critical set of early reading skills. It is also designed to be used by tutors in a valuable half-hour block of classroom time. We had to make difficult choices about what to include in the lessons. We encourage tutors to ask comprehension questions during the Book-Reading Time. We also assume that each student's classroom teacher is working on comprehension during classroom reading instruction and that comprehension will become a bigger emphasis in the student's reading instruction after early reading skills are mastered.

Vocabulary Instruction

Although there is not time for extended vocabulary instruction during a *Sound Partners* session, tutors can address vocabulary incidentally. This will become easier as tutors gain experience with the lessons.

Importantly, the tutor should notice when the student might not know the meaning of a word and use cues when the student cannot pronounce a word or use the word correctly in the phrasing of a sentence. Tutors won't be able to offer extended vocabulary instruction, but they will be able to provide brief vocabulary help.

Short, simple vocabulary instruction is suggested in the excellent book *Bringing Words to Life* (Beck, McKeown, & Kucan, 2002). These are good tips to review with tutors either at the initial training or at a follow-up training:

▶ **Choose** words that are useful, that are used frequently and in everyday speech. Also, choose words that are important for understanding one of the stories.

▶ **Tell** the meaning of the word in everyday language. Use an example in your definition.

For example, "A *plug* is something that closes a hole. Like a rag can be used to *plug* a hole in a bucket."

▶ **Ask** the student to use the word.

For example, "Tell me something about your life, and use the word *thud.*"

▶ **Involve** the student in the word.

For example, "If I said my hands were <u>chapped</u>, what might they look like?"

"If you had to <u>lug</u> a box up the steps, how might you feel?"

As the *Sound Partners* supervisor, you might extend vocabulary instruction in follow-up tutor training sessions or in tutor meetings. *Bringing Words to Life* includes other excellent vocabulary strategies for young readers.

Implementation Issues

Building Student Motivation

Sound Partners is an intensive program for young, struggling readers. Students spend 30 minutes a day and 4–5 days a week with their tutors. These are children for whom learning to read is hard work. It's not surprising that many students get discouraged at some point in the lessons and their energy flags. Supervisors and tutors can help prevent this and can encourage students when they need a boost. Remind tutors that the basic strategies for maintaining student success and motivation include:

▶ Maintaining a positive affect.

▶ Correcting errors immediately and positively.

▶ Noticing student accomplishments and providing specific praise.

▶ Consistently applying of rules for fingerpointing and rereading.

There are other strategies tutors can use to boost student motivation. Tutors should pay attention to what is motivating to their students. One student may love to show off her reading skills to the supervisor, the principal, or a parent. Another student may be highly motivated by marking a checklist to record his progress through the lessons. We have seen many students who like to look back at the words they read and spelled in earlier lessons and compare them to their current lesson words.

Within the lessons, each student will demonstrate strengths in some of the activities, and weakness in others. Tutors should praise the progress students make (e.g., "You really listen for all of those letter sounds—you always get the four-part segmenting right!"). Tutors need to know how effective praise can be in motivating their students. Students can be praised for providing the correct responses, reading smoothly and accurately, and correcting themselves. Students can also be praised for their efforts and attentiveness, even if their accuracy is less than perfect. Praise is important and motivating, but tutors shouldn't overdo it. Praise must be earned and sincere, or it will lose its effectiveness with students. Tutors have to make sure that praise is specific so that the student is aware of what she has done right.

Tutors should take advantage of naturally occurring opportunities during instruction to encourage, praise, and stimulate the student to work hard and do a little better each day.

Structuring the Tutoring Environment for Success

Each tutor, particularly if the tutor is a parent, will bring his or her own teaching style to the program. Tutors with varied teaching personalities have been very successful in the *Sound Partners* program. Regardless of their individual personalities, tutors all need basic strategies for managing students.

Organization and Pace

Tutors should have all their tutoring materials ready to use as soon as the student arrives. Tutors may need advice or modeling to keep the lessons going at a pace that keeps the student engaged and reduces gaps in instruction, during which the student gets distracted. Explain to tutors that good teachers often have a brisk pace for their instruction: not too fast for slower students, but with a momentum that maintains student interest.

Suggest that tutors consciously try to find a good pace for their tutoring. Tutors who understand and can find this optimal pace for instruction will have fewer behavior problems, and their students will be more engaged during the sessions. Learning to read is hard work for *Sound Partners* students. Tutors can help their students by observing the student carefully, responding to the student's errors and successes, and making the tutoring session a time of intense engagement in practicing critical reading skills.

Limiting Distractions

Students should not bring any toys or objects with them to tutoring, and the tutor should remove all distractions from the tutoring area. Even stray pencils and paper clips can distract a student, and the tutor will then need to bring the student's attention back to the lesson.

Setting Rules and Limits

Assure tutors that it's okay to set clear rules for the students to follow. Rules should be stated positively, as Do's, not as Don'ts. Rules should be simple and clear, so that tutor and student can easily know if a rule is being followed or ignored. Rules for tutoring might be:

▶ "At tutoring time, students always sit in their chairs with their feet on the ground."

▶ "During tutoring, it is your job to follow my directions."

▶ "During tutoring, the student always fingerpoints when reading."

The goal is to have as few rules as needed to manage student behavior. When a student breaks a rule, the tutor should enforce it by:

▶ Reminding the student what to do.

▶ Reinforcing the student for trying to comply.

▶ Modeling the desired behavior.

Sometimes tutors will need help with student behavior. We have taught tutors how to use a simple point system to reinforce compliant behavior. Stickers are good reinforcers for most first graders. We have also had success using a blank grid of boxes in which the student gets a stamped mark or a star for completing a difficult task, or for having a "good behavior" lesson. Then the colorful, completed, stamped chart goes home with the student when it is full. Very active students may need rules about talking or getting out of the chair. Tutors should know that they may need to set rules to make student expectations clear. When a student is silly or obnoxious, the tutor needs to understand the effectiveness of ignoring undesirable behaviors. Ignoring is a successful strategy in many situations.

The tutor asks . . .

What can I do if a student seems bored with the lessons?

Tutor affect and delivery of the lessons *strongly* influence a student's attitude towards the sessions. If student interest flags, tutors should try:

▶ Picking up the pace of the lessons.

▶ Being particularly attentive to the student's progress in reading stories, and praising the student's advances ("Wow, look at how easily you can read that page now, when it used to be so difficult!").

▶ Scaffolding instruction for a student with more serious reading problems. Tutors should always provide an opportunity for the student to be successful and provide assistance on difficult skills.

▶ Implementing a simple point system that rewards the student for completing each lesson or lesson part (using a mini-stamper and a grid of boxes).

Metacognitive Strategies

Researchers and educators have written about the value of having children understand the instructional goals we have for them and of helping them to think about what they are learning.

For example, in the Pair Practice component, the tutor can remind the student that many words contain letter pairs and that learning the pairs is a shortcut for reading these words. Tutors are trained and encouraged to point out sounds and words the student has learned when they appear in context; this is to impress upon the student the relation of the task he has been learning with the payoff—being able to use that skill to read a fun storybook, for example.

▶ "What letter pair is in that word?"

▶ "What letter pairs does couch contain?"

▶ "What letter pairs do you recognize on this page?"

Specific praise is another way of enhancing a student's awareness of what she is doing correctly:

▶ "You noticed that was a magic -e- word!"

▶ "You recognized your new sight word!"

▶ "You read that letter pair so well today—and yesterday it was very difficult for you!"

Reducing the Difficulty of Tasks

When a task is too difficult, the tutor should scaffold instruction to enable the student to complete part of the task. Suggestions for scaffolding tasks are included in descriptions of the individual lesson components.

Observing Tutors and Students

Tutor Implementation

Sound Partners is only as effective as the tutors who use it. A high degree of implementation fidelity is essential. This means that tutors must use the lessons as they are designed, without skipping or substituting components. The tutors must model the correct letter sounds, and the sounding-out strategy. Much of the field testing has involved finding effective instructional activities that tutors can use successfully. Furthermore, our research on tutor differences showed that students who had poor tutors did not differ at posttest from control students who did not receive *Sound Partners* tutoring.

You, as supervisor, must find a way to monitor tutor quality. This can be done by carefully selecting and hiring individuals who will be able to implement the instruction fully. Schools that hire experienced para-professionals may need to provide minimal supervision. Supervisors can improve the quality of tutoring by observing and coaching tutors to become more effective. Schools that hire tutors without previous teaching or reading experience will need to supervise and coach these tutors more closely.

In our research, the most effective tool in maintaining a high level of tutor fidelity has been the Tutor Observation Form (see the Appendix of the Tutor Handbook). We highly recommend that you use this form

to conduct your observations of tutors and to provide them with specific feedback on their instruction.

Using the Tutor Observation Form

All of the tutors at each site should have a copy of the Tutor Observation Form (available in the Tutor Handbook). The form clearly lists the critical features of each lesson component that they must demonstrate when they tutor a student. The supervisor circles a 1 or a 0 for every component observed during a session; a 1 is marked for correct implementation and a 0 is marked for incorrect implementation or if the component is skipped. The supervisor then adds the 1s and 0s together and divides by the total number of components. A score of less than 90% indicates that the tutor needs more specific feedback on his or her tutoring, or retraining in specific component delivery.

We recommend that you observe each tutor weekly during the first several months of tutoring. Later, you can observe each tutor monthly. File these Tutor Observation Forms so that they can be used to review tutor performance and improvement.

Things to Look For

In your role as supervisor, you should try to visit each tutor at least once a week. These visits need not be long, depending upon the skills of the tutor and the student's progress in the lessons. Within a week's time, however, a student can demonstrate behaviors that are difficult for a tutor to manage, or he or she may begin to get frustrated learning a specific skill. Tutors should not be left alone to handle these problems, and all tutors should be able to call their supervisor for assistance whenever needed. In our local *Sound Partners* sites, monthly tutor meetings with the supervisor have often been adequate. However new, less experienced tutors may initially require more frequent support.

1. When we observed tutoring sites, we first reviewed *tutoring logistics*:

   ▶ Is either the tutor or student absent? Does someone need to call the student's parents to find out when the student will return? If the tutor is absent, is a substitute tutor needed?

   ▶ Is the physical arrangement conducive to tutoring? Has the tutor been moved to a less desirable space? Are other school activities beginning to distract the tutor-student pair? Tutors with little previous experience working in schools may need someone to help them solve these logistical problems.

2. Next, we looked at the *dynamics of the tutor-student pair*:

   ▶ Is the tutor's affect positive and encouraging?

   ▶ Does the tutor need help managing a student who is reluctant to cooperate, bored, or refusing to follow the tutor's instructions?

3. We looked very closely at the *tutor's instruction*:

   ▶ Is the tutor following the lesson formats and training instructions?

   ▶ Is the tutor omitting parts of the lessons, or substituting her own materials?

   ▶ Is review of certain tutoring strategies needed? We used the Tutor Observation Form to collect and record data from tutor observations, and to share our observations with the tutors.

4. Finally, we looked closely at *student performance and progress* since last visit:

   ▶ Is the student consistently performing at 100% on all of the activities, and does he need to be moving more quickly or advanced to more challenging material?

   ▶ Is it apparent that the student has failed to master basic essential skills (such as letter sounds, magic -e- rule, sounding-out procedure) and needs to go back over and review these activities before going on? Or does the student need to continue to practice weaker skills while she continues forward in the lessons?

   ▶ Does the student need supplementary instruction to complement the lesson content? Does he need more practice with letter sounds or more practice with flash cards to learn sight words?

The Lesson Component Scope and Sequence chart (see Appendix) can be used by supervisors to anticipate tutor needs for storybooks that will be used in lessons. Supervisors can also use it to anticipate when a tutor will start to implement a new component and may need brief training or reminders of how to deliver the component correctly.

Sharing Feedback with Tutors

The Tutor Observation Form is a highly effective tool for collecting and sharing feedback with tutors on their instruction. The form captures tutor performance on the critical features of each lesson activity. As supervisor, you can share the form with a tutor immediately after an observation, or you can collect and summarize the observation data for each tutor. These data can be used for rehiring decisions or for assigning a tutor to another instructional program. You will find that you quickly come to know the best way to share feedback with each of your tutors. As tutors begin to use the lessons, interrupt them when needed to model or correct their instruction. It is important that tutors become comfortable getting feedback. Then, throughout the program, use modeling to correct tutors who are not following lesson directions, and to demonstrate techniques that would help a student who needed a slightly different strategy for learning. Make this as comfortable as possible for tutors by saying, "Here, let me try something with Chia." Modeling is often all that a tutor needs to correct or augment instruction.

You may *often* need to talk to individual tutors about the importance of using tutoring time for instruction rather than making friends with their students. When you notice that a tutor is using tutoring time for activities like drawing, reading library books, or other off-task activities, immediately talk to the tutor and emphasize the need to maximize instructional time. Emphasize the importance of using the tutoring opportunity to advance the student's skills as much as possible.

For some problems, it is more effective to set aside time at the beginning or end of the lesson to problem solve with the tutor (without the student present). Sometimes this will relate to lesson content. For example, a student may have great difficulty learning how to decode, and the tutor may need help with strategies to encourage the student. Sometimes problems relate to the tutor's inefficient use of valuable tutoring time. In this case, a meeting can be used to think about ways to organize materials and tutoring set-up so that less time is wasted.

Sometimes modeling the desired tutoring behaviors doesn't work, and a tutor needs private, direct feedback. This is absolutely necessary if a tutor berates a student or uses other inappropriate feedback and student management strategies. It is also necessary if a tutor deviates from the lesson format or needs individual retraining in a tutoring skill, such as sound blending. The students that *Sound Partners* serves are those least likely to acquire reading skills without systematic and explicit instruction. It is critical to monitor and coach tutors to help them provide this instruction.

The supervisor asks . . .

What can I do if a tutor is very negative with a student?

Sound Partners tutoring should be a positive, happy part of the student's day. Most students love to come and work with "their" tutors. When a tutor uses inappropriate or negative reinforcement with a student you can:

▶ Model appropriate tutoring behavior, showing the tutor areas in which the student was doing well and praising the student for both success and effort.

▶ Take the tutor aside and discuss the importance of positive feedback for students who are struggling with beginning reading skills. Explain how discouraging it is for students to be told, "You're not trying," or, "No—that's wrong!" and thastudents must never be discouraged this way. Explain that the tutor's role is to acknowledge and praise the student's efforts, to record student performance in the lessons, and to point out student progress. It's highly motivating to a student to see that last week he got two out of six words correct, and this week he got five out of six words correct!

If you notice that a tutor is having negative interactions with a student, carefully observe that tutor. If needed, provide repeated feedback. And, if necessary, tell the tutor that you have to let her go because she isn't able to provide the consistency of support that the students need in this program. Because some schools find it difficult to recruit tutors, they may be reluctant to let a tutor go. We have found in our research that poor tutoring is harmful and removes students from skilled classroom reading instruction. You must be alert for tutors who should be let go, due to either inappropriate, negative affect or to poor instruction.

For more help with tutor coaching, see the guidelines in the Tutor Handbook under Error Correction and Specific Praise, as well as those on Student Behavior Management. You should also encourage your tutors to use the Tutor Self-Check Quiz in the Tutor Handbook; it's a great way for them to monitor their understanding of basic *Sound Partners* strategies.

Monitoring Progress

Schools need efficient, reliable ways to be sure that tutors and students are making maximum progress in the lessons. Supervisors cannot be with each tutor every tutoring day. Other ways are used to provide a picture of student progress.

Mastery Tests
The tutor or supervisor can administer a set of curriculum-based Mastery Tests every ten lessons; student copies of the tests are placed at intervals throughout the lessons. The tests check student mastery of skills taught in the previous lessons. Students who test at less than 90% mastery may need to be moving a bit slower through the lessons, or may need to go back and review specific skills. Students who test at 100% may be able to move more quickly or skip lessons until they are working on material at their instructional level.

As a *Sound Partners* supervisor, you may not have time to administer all of the mastery tests yourself. In these cases, the tutors partner among themselves and test each other's students. One tutor will let her partner know that she will be completing Lesson 10 or 20 today. The partner will then make arrangements to test the other tutor's student as soon as convenient. If no other arrangements can be made, tutors should test their own students; however, it is better if someone else does the testing.

Tutors should always review their students' Mastery Tests—if possible with their supervisor. You should file and retain completed Mastery Tests and likewise review them and provide feedback that seems appropriate. Mastery Tests may also be shared with a student's classroom teacher to inform him or her of the student's progress.

Coordinating with Classroom Teachers
Sound Partners tutors most often work with students during the school day, and they rarely have opportunities to talk to their students' classroom teachers. Sometimes tutors and teachers discuss students' reading development before or after school. When teachers know what skills the tutor is working on, they can often reinforce those skills during their classroom instruction.

Some of our *Sound Partners* field-test schools have incorporated the program into their building's reading program. In these schools, *Sound Partners* tutors prepare quarterly reports on student progress. These reports are used by teachers for parent conferences and progress assessment. The tutors also participate in conferences on their students' progress or placement. One simple means of sharing information with teachers is through the *Sound Partners* mastery tests that include the letter sounds and most of the words that the student has learned to read and spell. If tutors are teaching to 90–95% mastery criteria, the student should be able to read and spell most of the words on these tests. The tests will give teachers a snapshot of the types of words the student is currently learning. Some teachers may want to incorporate these words in spelling quizzes or in peer-tutoring review/practice sessions.

Training Tutors

We recommend that tutors who will be using the *Sound Partners* program receive one half-day of initial training, and an average of one day of follow-up training as needed. Follow-up training may be provided throughout the year to introduce new tutoring components and to reinforce and review basic strategies. The follow-up training is flexible and should be planned as needed to match individual site needs.

Tutor Training Outline for Initial Training

Before the training begins, you or another supervisor should set up the space and materials. If it is a small group of tutors, the training might occur around a conference table. With a larger group of tutors, tables or desks should be organized so that the trainees can sit together to practice in pairs.

Begin the initial training, as the Tutor Training Outline that follows indicates, by setting out a sign-in sheet, nametags, and handouts near the door or front of the room. Once group members arrive, have people introduce themselves.

Trainers will provide the trainees with Tutor Handbooks, which include sample lesson pages. The trainees can use the sample lessons to refer to when the trainer models each component, and when the trainees pair up and practice the tutor and student roles for each lesson component.

Tutor Training Outline for Initial Training

I. Introduction

    A. Business

        1. As people arrive, they sign training log, get nametags, sit in pairs.

        2. Schedule for the day.

    B. Overview of Sound Partners Program

    C. Training Overview

        1. Skilled tutoring requires knowledge of content and methodology.

        2. Today's training:

            ▶ Emphasis on tutor/student content and methodology.

            ▶ Addresses methodology by modeling it (explain, model, practice, feedback, review).

            ▶ All tutor trainees must demonstrate proficiency in basic *Sound Partners* components by the end of training session.

II. Sound Partners Instructional Methodology

    A. Systematic *(Lesson Component Scope and Sequence)*

        1. Introduce new sounds/skills gradually—about one sound introduced per lesson.

        2. Provide cumulative practice and review

        3. Teach letter-sound correspondences and decoding/encoding (reading/spelling) of letters/sounds, words, sentences, and connected text (paragraphs, etc.).

    B. Direct

        1. Model (show).

        2. Scaffold (provide needed help and small steps so that the student can have success and move towards independent mastery of the reading skill).

        3. Practice with feedback, letting the student know how she is doing (refer to Tutor Handbook's section on Error Correction and Specific Praise).

            ▶ Provide error correction.

            ▶ Give specific praise.

            ▶ Avoid negative comments.

            ▶ Provide extra practice.

    C. Consistent

        1. Lesson format is predictable.

        2. Clear expectations for student behavior (e.g., fingerpointing, rereading sentences with an error).

III. The Lessons

    A. Overview of Components (Sound Partners *lesson components—short, varied, engaging activities to teach skills)*

Continued ➙

B. Close Look—explain, model, practice (Sound Partners *sample lesson*)

C. General Lesson Format

1. Tutor directions in right-hand column, student works off left-hand area.

2. Student sits on the left of tutor, facing the student portion of the lesson.

3. Items (letters, pairs, and words) in box means that the tutor models these new items.

4. A pencil icon means that the student writes/spells on paper.

D. Individual Lesson Components

1. **Say the Sounds**

   ▶ *Explain*: Tutor models new sounds in box. Keywords are found on Letter Sounds Cards and in Tutor Handbook.

   ▶ *Model*: Fingerpointing, working left to right, error correction using keyword and/or model, extra practice, specific praise, using new/difficult sounds, giving sounds instead of letter names.

   ▶ *Model*: How each letter sound is made (articulated).

2. **Segmenting**

   ▶ *Explain*: Auditory (hearing, listening) nature of the task, going from three- to four-part box.

   ▶ *Model*: Repeating the word, pointing to boxes while saying sounds, sweeping finger and saying whole word.

   ▶ *Model*: Error correction—tutor models, student repeats, or tutor scaffolds (tutor says each sound while student points, student repeats).

3. **Word Reading**

   ▶ *Explain*: Sounding out, not stopping between sounds. Early lessons look different, include arrows. Practice identifying beginning, end, middle sounds. Spelling to practice difficult words.

   ▶ *Model*: Sounding out, error correction—directing student to difficult part of word, allowing student to self-correct, specific praise, spelling correction.

4. **Sight Words**

   ▶ *Explain*: Sight words difficult to sound out, learned by remembering sequence of letters. Spelling aloud while looking at word as a learning tool.

   ▶ *Model*: Error correction not by using letter sounds but by supplying the word and having student say and spell it.

5. **Sentence Reading**

   ▶ *Model*: Fingerpointing, error correction, rereading, and specific praise.

6. **Magic -e-**

   ▶ *Explain*: Magic -e- rule, correct by reminding student of rule. Use the words/steps provided for corrections.

Continued →

7. **Word Endings**

   ▶ *Explain/Model*: Endings taught to allow students to *read* words (no spelling rules yet). Don't say ending in isolation.

8. **Pair Practice**

   ▶ *Explain*: Use of chunks in word decoding.

   ▶ *Model*: Remind student to look for letter pairs, have student find/read pair first, then whole word.

9. **Reading Long Words**

   ▶ *Explain*: Strategies for finding/reading chunks of word, then reading whole word.

   ▶ *Model*: Chunking compound words, inflected words, words with affixes.

10. **Book Reading**

    ▶ *Explain*: Reading time, book selection steps, reading method selection, error correction, and two rules for students (fingerpoint, reread).

E. *Review of Error Correction Strategies*

1. **For a decodable word:**

   ▶ "What's the first sound?"

   ▶ "What does the <u>ai</u> pair say?"

   ▶ "That sound is /b/—try it again."

2. **For a sight word:**

   ▶ "That's a sight word."

   ▶ "That word is _____. You say it and spell it."

> **Tutors pair up and practice each component.**
>
> Trainer uses Initial Tutor Training Checklist (see Appendix) to confirm that each trainee has mastered basic criteria.

IV. Instructional and Behavioral Management

A. *Use of Time* (Sound Partners *lesson components*)

1. Full 30 minutes.
2. Brisk pace.
3. Smooth transitions.
4. Stay on-task.

B. *Behavior Management*

1. Set ground rules.
2. Maintain positive affect.
3. Student success breeds good behavior (consistency, scaffolding, positive error correction, specific praise).

End ◀

Follow-up Training

It is unproductive to try to cram into one session *all* the skills that tutors will need to use *Sound Partners*. We recommend that you plan a half-day initial training to cover the basic components. Then schedule a second follow-up session soon after to cover the rest of the lesson components and to address questions tutors will have once they begin tutoring. The supervisor should schedule follow-up training based on his observations (use the Follow-up Tutor Training Proficiency Checklist in the Appendix). Topics that often need to be addressed in follow-up training with tutors are:

▶ How to teach sound blending correctly.

▶ How to read compound words.

▶ How to teach word endings.

▶ How to teach letter-pair reading and spelling.

▶ Magic -e- instruction and correction.

Incidental tutor training should occur throughout the tutoring sessions as the supervisor observes each tutor during instruction and as tutors express the need to review and discuss aspects of instruction.

Handwriting—Often tutors and teachers wonder how much time tutors should spend correcting student handwriting. While there will not be enough time in the 30-minute *Sound Partners* block to provide intensive handwriting intervention, tutors can provide incidental modeling and correction to help students develop good handwriting habits. This can be a topic for a follow-up training. You can provide tutors with the handwriting chart used by the classroom teachers. The Handwriting Lessons program in the *Process Assessment of the Learner (PAL) Intervention Kit* (Berninger, 1998) includes a laminated chart that illustrates with numbered arrow cues the order and direction of pencil strokes for forming each letter of the alphabet. If a student is inefficiently drawing rather than writing his letters, the tutor can prompt the student to begin forming the letter at the top rather than the bottom of the letter. The tutor can also prompt the student to use an effective pencil grip. As tutors become more comfortable with the *Sound Partners* lessons, they can add corrections and modeling in handwriting during the spelling tasks. Tutors should use classroom primary writing paper for the spelling tasks in the *Sound Partners* lessons. This lined paper will help beginning writers form their letters correctly.

Vocabulary—*Sound Partners* tutors will work with many students with a limited vocabulary. These include students with limited English proficiency, and students from lower SES backgrounds or with limited language experience. Tutors may wonder how much time they should take to develop vocabulary knowledge. Tutors can be most effective by noticing when the student encounters a word that is not in his vocabulary. For example, this often happens with students reading the *Bob* books that include the words "keg" and "jig." When this happens, the tutor should not ignore the word, but neither should the tutor get bogged down in defining it. The tutor should simply provide a short definition (e.g., "That's a small wooden barrel," or "That's a little dance") or use the word in a simple sentence.

Conclusion

In this handbook we have outlined the information that supervisors need in order to oversee a *Sound Partners* tutoring program in their building. *Sound Partners* supervisors should certainly be thoroughly familiar with the lesson components in order to train tutors and provide ongoing feedback on their instruction. Like all research-based interventions, the care with which tutors use the program strongly predicts student outcomes. You can ensure that the tutors at your site deliver the highest quality tutoring by carefully recruiting tutors; providing the recommended half-day initial training, with modeling and practice, in all lesson components; and coaching tutors once they begin to use the program with their students.

Well-trained and supervised tutors help their students attain the critical early reading skills targeted in the lessons while also developing their own skills in beginning reading instruction. The most skilled parent-tutors in our field-test sites have tutored for up to six years because they find their work so rewarding and reinforcing. They have developed a deep understanding of early reading acquisition and see the results of their instruction in their students' progress.

The investment that you, as *Sound Partners* supervisor, make in recruitment, training, and supervision of the tutors at your school has long-term benefits for students. We welcome feedback from teachers and supervisors who use *Sound Partners*, and we hope that our work on *Sound Partners* enables others to reach the struggling readers in their schools.

Glossary

Alphabetic Principle

The underlying assumption that each speech sound (phoneme) in a language should have its own graphic representation (grapheme).

Automaticity

Fluent performance without conscious deployment of attention.

Components

The different skill sections that make up each *Sound Partners* lesson.

Compound Words

A combination of two or more words that function as a single word.

Comprehension

The part of the reading process that focuses on meaning.

Consonant Blend

Two or more consonants that appear together in a word, each consonant retaining its own sound.

Consonant Sound

A sound in which the airflow is cut off either partially or completely when the sound is produced.

Continuous Sound

A sound that can be drawn out, e.g., /m/ or /s/.

Controlled Text

Text that is chosen or written to be readable for a student with a given set of reading skills.

Decodable Text

Text that a student can read using word-attack (decoding) skills that are in the student's repertoire. Usually refers to text containing mostly words that can be "sounded out."

Decoding

Ability to translate a word from print to speech (reading) by sounding it out.

Encoding

Ability to translate a word from speech to print (spelling).

Expository Text

Text that reports factual information.

Feedback

Information given to the student about his/her performance.

Fingerpointing

Use of a finger to track letters, letter pairs, and words while reading.

Fluency

Ability to read with sufficient speed and accuracy to support comprehension.

Grapheme

The written representation of a phoneme (sound), as in a letter or group of letters.

Keyword

A word chosen to function as a reminder or example of a particular sound or blend of sounds.

Model

To show or demonstrate for the student.

Narrative Text

Text that tells a story.

Orthography

A writing system.

Phoneme

The smallest unit of sound found in speech.

Phoneme Awareness

Ability to hear, identify, and manipulate individual sounds in the spoken language.

Phonics

The study of the relationship between letters and the sounds they represent.

Phonological Awareness

An umbrella term that covers an understanding of the sounds of language. This includes sound/word rhyming, blending, segmentation, deletion, and substitution.

Rime

The part of a word or syllable that includes the vowel and what follows it.

Scaffolding

Providing needed help in weak areas so that the student can have success while moving toward independent mastery of a skill.

Scope and Sequence

Information about the content and order of skill-set introduction.

Segmenting (phoneme)

Dividing a word into separate phonemes.

Sight Word

A word that does not follow a regular phonetic spelling pattern.

Specific Praise

Praise that states exactly which part/aspect of a response/ behavior was completed correctly or successfully.

Stop Sound

Sound formed by closing or blocking off the airflow and then exploding a puff of air, e.g., /b/, /p/, and /t/.

Word Family

A group of words sharing a common rime.

Vowel Sound

A sound in which the airflow is not obstructed when the sound is made.

Bibliography

This list includes books and articles that were foundations for *Sound Partners*, as well as useful resources for *Sound Partners* supervisors.

Adams, M. (1990). *Beginning to read: Thinking and learning about print.* Cambridge, MA: MIT.

Beck, I. L., McKeown, M. G., & Kucan, L. (2002). *Bringing words to life: Robust vocabulary instruction.* New York, NY: Guilford Press.

Berninger, V. (1998). *Process assessment of the learner (PAL): Intervention kit.* San Antonio, TX: The Psychological Corporation.

Carnine, D., Silbert, J., & Kameenui, E. (1990). *Direct instruction reading.* Englewood Cliffs, NJ: Prentice-Hall.

Ehri, L. C. (1998). Grapheme-phoneme knowledge is essential for learning to read words in English. In J. L. Metsala & L. C. Ehri (Eds.), *Word recognition in beginning literacy* (pp. 3–40). Mahwah, NJ: Erlbaum.

Foorman, B. R., Francis, D. J., Beeler, T., Winikates, D., & Fletcher, J. M. (1997). Early interventions for children with reading problems: Study designs and preliminary findings. *Learning Disabilities, 8,* 63–71.

Iversen, S., & Tunmer, W. E. (1993). Phonological processing skills and reading recovery program. *Journal of Educational Psychology, 85,* 112–126.

Kuhn, M. R., & Stahl, S. A. (2003). Fluency: A review of developmental and remedial practices. *Journal of Educational Psychology, 95,* 3–21.

Juel, C. (1996). What makes literacy tutoring effective? *Reading Research Quarterly, 30,* 268–289.

Moats, L. (1995). *Spelling: Development, disability, and instruction.* Timonium, MD: York.

Moats, L. (2000). *Speech to print: Language essentials for teachers.* Baltimore: Brookes.

National Reading Panel. (2000). *Teaching children to read: An evidence-based assessment of the scientific research literature on reading and its implications for reading instruction: Reports of the subgroups.* Bethesda, MD: National Institute of Child Health and Human Development.

National Research Council (1998). *Preventing reading difficulties in young children.* Washington, DC: National Academy Press.

Sprick, R., Garrison, M., & Howard, L. (2000). *Para Pro: Supporting the instructional process.* Longmont, CO: Sopris West Educational Services.

The following references describe our research on *Sound Partners*:

Jenkins, J. R., Peyton, J. A., Sanders, E. A., & Vadasy, P. F. (2004). Effects of reading decodable texts in supplemental first-grade tutoring. *Scientific Studies of Reading, 8*, 53–85.

Jenkins, J. R., Vadasy, P. F., Firebaugh, M., & Profilet, C. (2000). Tutoring first-grade struggling readers in phonological reading skills. *Learning Disabilities Research and Practice, 15*, 75–84.

Vadasy, P. F., Jenkins, J. R., Antil, L. R., Wayne, S. K., & O'Connor, R. E. (1997). The effectiveness of one-to-one tutoring by community tutors for at-risk beginning readers. *Learning Disabilities Quarterly, 20*, 126–139.

Vadasy, P. F., Jenkins, J. R., Antil, L. R., Wayne, S. K., & O'Connor, R. E. (1997). Community-based early reading intervention for at-risk first graders. *Learning Disabilities Research and Practice, 12*, 29–39.

Vadasy, P. F., Jenkins, J. R., & Pool, K. (2000). Effects of tutoring in phonological and early reading skills on students at risk for reading disabilities. *Journal of Learning Disabilities, 33*, 579–590.

Vadasy, P. F., Sanders, E. A., Peyton, J. A., & Jenkins, J. R. (2003). Timing and intensity of tutoring: A closer look at the conditions for effective early literacy tutoring. *Learning Disabilities Research and Practice, 17*, 227–241.

Sound Partners Reading Books

All books are published by Scholastic.

Bob Books, written by Bobby Lynn Maslen and illustrated by John Maslen, are a wonderful series of boxed, phonics-based storybooks for beginning readers.

Bob Books: First! (Level A, Set 1) (1976, rev. 2000)

Mat

Sam

Dot

Mac

Dot and the Dog

Dot and Mit

Jig and Mag

Muff and Ruff

10 Cut Ups

Peg and Ted

Lad and the Fat Cat

The Vet

Bob Books: Fun! (Level A, Set 2) (1999)

Fun in the Sun

Up Pup

Pip and Pog

The Big Hat

Bow Wow

Go Bus

The Red Hen

Sox the Fox

The Sad Cat

Rub a Dub

OK Kids

0 to 10

Bob Books: Plus! (Level B, Set 1) (1996)

Kittens

Floppy Mop

Summer

Lolly Pops

The Red Car

Frogs

Funny Bunny

Bed Bugs

Bob Books: Pals! (Level B, Set 2) (1987, rev. 2000)

Ten Men

Bump

The Swimmers

Cat and Mouse

Max and the Tom Cats

Willy's Wish

Jumper and the Clown

Samantha

Bob Books: Wow! (Level C, Set 1) (1987, rev. 2000)

Bud's Nap

The Game

Joe's Toe

The Picnic

The King

The Train

Chickens

The Visit

The Class Trip (1999) by Grace Maccarone

The Big Red Sled (2001) by Jane E. Gerver

Shipwreck Saturday (1998) by Bill Cosby

Poppleton and Friends (1997) by Cynthia Rylant

Poppleton Forever (1998) by Cynthia Rylant

Appendix

Lesson Component Scope and Sequence

Sound Partners

COMPONENTS	LESSONS 1	2	3	4	5	6	7	8	9	10
New Letter Sounds/ Pairs	a, m	s	t	Review	c	d	n	o	Review	h
Say the Sounds (and Write Sounds)	[a], m	a, m, [s]	a, m, s, [t]	a, m, s, t	a, [c], m, s, t	a, c, [d], m, s, t	a, c, d, m, [n], s, t	a, c, d, m, n, [o], s, t	a, c, d, m, n, o, s, t	a, c, d, [h], m, n, o, s, t
Segmenting	3-part	3-part	3-part	3-part	3-part	3-part	3-part	3-part	3-part	3-part
Word Reading (and Spelling)*	am	am, Sam	at, mat, sat, tam	Review	Cam, cat, Mac	cad, mad, sad, Tad	ad, and, Dan, tan	cot, dad, Dot, mom, nod, not, on, sod, Tom	con	cod, had, ham, hat, hot
Book Reading						*Mat* Bob Books A-1			*Sam* Bob Books A-1	

*Only newly introduced words listed.

Lesson Component Scope and Sequence

COMPONENTS	|	LESSONS 11	12	13	14	15	16	17	18	19	20
New Letter Sounds/ Pairs		g	r	b	Review	i	Review	Review	p	w	j
Say the Sounds (and Write Sounds)		a, c, d, g , h, m, n, o, s, t	a, c, d, g, h, m, n, o, r , s, t	a, b , c, d, g, h, m, n, o, r, s, t	a, b, c, g, h, m, n, o, r, t	a, b, c, g, h, i , m, n, o, r, s	a, b, c, d, g, i, m, n, o, r, t	a, b, c, d, g, h, i, m, n, o, r, s, t	a, b, c, d, g, h, i, n, o, p , r	a, b, c, d, h, i, o, p, t, w	a, b, d, g, i, j , m, n, p, r, s, w
Segmenting		3-part	3-part	3-part	3-part	3-part	3-part	3-part	3-part	3-part	3-part
Word Reading (and Spelling)*		cog, got, nag, sag, tag	hog, Nat, rag, ran, rat	bag, ban, bat, bog, cab, mob, nab, sob	bad, Mag	bin, dig, dim, hit, in, it, sit, tin	big, can, dab, hid, rid, rig	did, dog, Mit	bop, dip, hop, map, mop, nap, pan, pig, pin, pit, pot, ram, rap, rip	cap, pad, pat, wag, wig, win, wit	jam, jig, Jim, job, jog, jot
Sight Words		a, The	Review	in	as, has	Review	his, is	isn't	of	you	to
Book Reading		*Sam* Bob Books A-1	*Dot* Bob Books A-1		*Mac* Bob Books A-1		*Dot and the Dog* Bob Books A-1		*Dot and Mit* Bob Books A-1		*Jig and Mag* Bob Books A-1

*Only newly introduced words listed.

Sound Partners

Lesson Component Scope and Sequence

Sound Partners

COMPONENTS	LESSONS									
	21	22	23	24	25	26	27	28	29	30
New Letter Sounds/ Pairs	u	Review	f	Review	e	Review	th	k	l	x
Say the Sounds (and Write Sounds)	a, b, d, h, i, j, n, p, r, [u], w	a, d, h, i, j, n, p, r, u, w	b, [f], i, j, n, p, r, s, u, w	a, d, f, g, i, j, p, r, s, t, u, w	a, b, d, [e], f, j, m, n, t, u, w	b, c, d, e, f, j, p, r, s, t, u	a, b, e, f, h, i, o, r, t, u, w, [th]	a, e, f, g, j, [k], n, p, t, u, th	d, e, f, g, i, [l], k, r, w, th	d, e, f, g, j, k, l, o, p, u, [x], th
Segmenting	3-part	3-part	3-part	3-part	3-part	4-part	4-part	4-part	4-part	4-part
Word Reading (and Spelling)*	bud, bug, cup, cut, dud, hug, jug, jut, pup, rib, up	bun, rim, rub, run	fad, fan, fat, fig, fin, fit, fun, Muff, Ruff	fog, huff, puff, rot	fed, men, pet, red, rug, tug, wet	dug, hen, jet, nut, pet, rub, sap, tip	bath, bib, fed, get, net, path, pen, rut, that, then, thin	dub, gum, keg, kid, Kim, Kip, kit, than, this	fell, let, lid, log, lop, lot, mill, pill	box, fix, fox, mix, set, six
Sight Words*	Review	Review	for, or	can't, didn't	come, some	into	were	be, he, me, we	said	it's, let's
Word Endings	[s]	s	s	s						
Book Reading	Jig and Mag Bob Books A-1		Muff and Ruff Bob Books A-1		10 Cut Ups Bob Books A-1		Peg and Ted Bob Books A-1		Lad and the Fat Cat Bob Books A-1	
Supplementary Reading					Fun in the Sun Bob Books A-1		Up Pup Bob Books A-1		Pip and Pog Bob Books A-1	

Lesson Component Scope and Sequence

LESSONS

COMPONENTS	31	32	33	34	35	36	37	38	39	40
New Letter Sounds/Pairs	Review	v	y	z	sh	Review	ch	Review	Review	wh
Say the Sounds (and Write Sounds)	a, c, e, f, i, k, l, o, s, t, u, x, th	a, b, e, h, i, j, u, k, l, [v], x, th	a, e, i, k, l, n, s, t, v, x, [y], th	e, i, l, o, r, t, u, v, x, y, [z], th	d, e, f, i, k, o, p, u, v, x, y, z, [sh]	a, c, e, h, l, o, s, t, u, v, w, y, z, sh	b, h, i, j, o, u, v, x, y, z, [ch], sh	e, h, i, j, l, n, t, u, y, z, ch, sh	a, e, g, i, l, o, r, u, v, x, y, z, ch, sh	d, e, k, l, n, t, x, y, z, ch, th, [wh]
Segmenting	4-part	4-part	4-part	4-part	4-part	4-part	4-part			
Word Reading (and Spelling)*	bun, lip, lot, met, Ned, nub	lug, van, vat, vet, vex	yap, yak, yen, yes, yet, yup	fax, fizz, fuzz, jazz, leg, sip, zam, zap, zig, zip	band, bus, buzz, fish, lag, mash, rash, shed, shop, web	bash, dish, hand, land, lash, math, sand, shin, shot	bent, chat, chin, chip, chop, rich, sent, such, tent	dash, sham, shut, wish	best, blob, clip, flag, flip, nest, ship, slum, stop, west	hush, wham, when, whim, whip
Inside-Sound Spelling									✓starts	✓
Sight Words	was	they	I, I'll, I'm	all	Review	there	you'll	what, what's	Review	saw
Word Endings										
Book Reading	Lad and the Fat Cat Bob Books A-1	The Big Hat Bob Books A-2		The Vet Bob Books A-1		Bow-Wow Bob Books A-2		Ten Men Bob Books B-2		The Red Hen Bob Books A-2
Supplementary Reading								Go Bus Bob Books A-2		

*Only newly introduced words listed.

Lesson Component Scope and Sequence

LESSONS

COMPONENTS	41	42	43	44	45	46	47	48	49	50
New Letter Sounds/Pairs	Review	Review	qu, fl, sk, sl	Review	er	sw	ee, st	ck	ou, tr	ue
Say the Sounds (and Write Sounds)	a, c, g, i, l, o, r, y, z, ch, sh, wh	c, d, e, i, l, o, p, u, v, w, x, y, ch, sh, wh	b, f, g, l, p, x, y, ch, [fl], [qu], [sk], [sl], th, wh	a, e, f, i, v, w, y, ch, fl, qu, sh, sk, sl, th, wh	a, b, h, i, l, o, u, y, z, ch, [er], qu, sk, wh	h, i, n, u, w, ch, er, fl, qu, sh, sk, sl, [sw], wh	g, i, l, p, r, x, z, ch, [ee], er, qu, [st], sw	a, d, e, h, o, p, ch, [ck], ee, er, qu, sh, sl, st, sw, wh	c, l, u, v, w, ch, ck, ee, er, [ou], sw, [tr]	j, t, y, ck, ee, er, ou, qu, sw, tr, [ue], wh
Word Reading (and Spelling)*	chap, gosh, much, mush, plan, plug, rent, shell, stag, with	lump, pump, shim, shod, step, stub, wax	quit, quilt, quiz, flash, flip, linked, pumped, skims, slash, task	chaps, chimp, skid, skips, them, thud	Bert, bumper, chill, crunched, faster, fern, helper, her, hunter, letter, robin, skips, stern	ask, herder, mask, slipper, slump, stands, swims, swish, whiz	cheeks, feed, feel, glee, lifted, need, sheen, sleep, steel, steep, stone, sweeps, went	bee, chilly, feet, free, heel, heel, lock, luck, quack, queen, quick, rancher	couch, hound, licked, limps, ouch, outer, round, rusty, shouted, south, straps, tricked, trout	blue, cloudy, clue, coffee, deeper, due, glue, ground, noun, pouch, sifter, sixteen, thunder
Sight Words*	over	Review	she, she's	Review	Review	want	by, my	Review	house, mouse	Review
Inside-Sound Spelling	✓	✓								
Spelling Similar Sounds									[ch], [tr]	ch, tr
Magic -e-						✓ starts	✓	✓	✓	✓
Word Endings		[ed] with /t/ sound	[ed] with /d/ sound	[ed] with /ed/ sound	ed (all)	[y]	y	y		y
Final m and n Blends			✓ starts	✓	✓	✓	✓	✓	✓	✓
Pair Practice			✓ starts	✓	✓	✓	✓	✓	✓	✓
Book Reading	Sox the Fox Bob Books A-2	Kittens Bob Books B-1		Rub a Dub Bob Books A-2		Bump Bob Books B-2		The Swimmers Bob Books B-2		Summer Bob Books B-1
Supplementary Reading		The Sad Cat Bob Books A-2		OK Kids Bob Books A-2		0-10 Bob Books A-2		Floppy Mop Bob Books B-1		Lolly Pops Bob Books B-1

*Only newly introduced words listed.

Sound Partners

Lesson Component Scope and Sequence

LESSONS

COMPONENTS	51	52	53	54	55	56	57	58	59	60
New Letter Sounds/Pairs	ew	Review	-y /ī/	Review	ar	Review	Review	ow	Review	al
Say the Sounds (and Write Sounds)	l, n, ck, ee, er, [ew], ou, qu, sl, sk, ue	ch, ck, ee, er, ew, ou, qu, sh, th, ue, wh	ck, er, ew, ou, qu, th, ue, [-y]	ch, ck, ee, er, ew, ou, qu, sh, ue, wh, -y	[ar], ck, ee, er, ew, ou, wh, -y	ar, ch, ck, ee, er, ew, ou, sh, th, wh, -y	ar, ch, ck, fl, ee, ew, [gr], ou, qu, sh, sn, th, tr	ar, ck, ee, ew, ou, [ow], ue, -y	ar, ck, er, ew, gr, ou, ow, ue	[al], ar, ck, ee, ew, ou, ow, ue, wh
Word Reading (and Spelling)*	cloud, crew, dew, drew, found, indeed, new, our, out, sound, stew, weeds	flew, flip, flop, flour, grew, quacks, slam, slap, snap, true, wheels	cry, dry, my, newer, shy, sky, supply	chew, litter, loud, newest, rounder, track, tricked, try	barn, hard, slick, tart, tricked, white, why, yarn	darker, grime, jar, market, parking, same, scar, slouch, start, threw, whine	flicker, green, grin, outing, quart, sharp, snack, snout, stewing	arm, army, artist, brow, chart, chow, flower, plow, power, spark, started, wow	arch, ark, barking, charm, how, howl, shower, starter, tower	ball, brighter, calm, crowd, farmer, harp, high, now, salty, stall
Sight Words*	any, many	head	knew	know	have	Review	one, two	live	very	says
Spelling Similar Sounds	ch, tr									
Useful Word Chunks							[igh]	[ight]	Review	
Magic -e-	✓	✓	✓	✓	✓	✓	✓	✓	✓	✓
Word Endings					[ing]	ing	y			ing
Long u Sounds			✓starts	✓	✓	✓				
Pair Practice	✓	✓	✓	✓	✓	✓	✓nonwords	✓nonwords	✓nonwords	✓nonwords
Book Reading	*Summer* Bob Books B-1	*Cat and Mouse* Bob Books B-2		*Bud's Nap* Bob Books C-1		*The Red Car* Bob Books B-1		*Max and the Tom Cats* Bob Books B-2	*Willy's Wish* Bob Books B-2	
Supplementary Reading	*Lolly Pops* Bob Books B-1									*Frogs* Bob Books B-1

*Only newly introduced words listed.

46 Implementation Manual

Sound Partners

Lesson Component Scope and Sequence

COMPONENTS	61	62	63	64	65	66	67	68	69	70
New Letter Sounds/Pairs	Review	ay	Review	oo/oo	Review	oa	Review	ai	Review	ea
Say the Sounds (and Write Sounds)	ai, ar, ee, er, ew, ou, ow, ue	ai, ar, [ay], ew, ow	ai, ar, ay, er, ew, ou, ow, th, ue	ar, ay, er, ew, [oo/oo], ou, ow, ue	ai, ar, ay, ch, er, ee, ew, oo/oo, ou, ow, qu, sh, th, ue, wh	ai, ay, ew, [oa], oo/oo, ow	ai, ay, ew, oa, oo/oo, ou	[ai], ar, ay, er, ew, oa, oo, ou	ai, ai, ar, ay, ee, er, ew, oa, oo, ou, ow, ue	ai, ai, ay, [ea], ee, oa, oo
Word Reading (and Spelling)*	archer, ballgame, bright, brown, carpet, outfit, outside, scald, sheets, sparkler, sunshine, taller	clay, daytime, highest, marker, payday, pinball, play, smart, stray, target	always, frighten, intern, marker, owl, playground, perky, skate, sprayed, staying, sticky, thing	boots, brewing, cartoons, clerk, farming, hook, mighty, outside, room, shook, stewing, Sue, tar, troops	charts, crook, frowning, harsh, hood, layer, mark, quicker, thick, tighten, took, tooth, white	floated, frowning, lighter, malted, roasted, slight, soapy, toasty, wallet	bars, cooled, foamy, lumpy, mushy, pray, right, roasted, stamp, stood, swaying, toasted	days, failed, jail, mail, mermaid, paid, plain, rain, sailing, temper, tighten, waiting, way	away, brain, claim, flight, frogs, gray, noon, painted, stain, strainer, trail, tools	beans, dealer, heated, lean, meanest, painter, sea, sealed, slightly, team, trailer, train, tray, treated, yeast
Sight Words	Review	don't	Review	their	we'll, we've	who	eyes, from	are, aren't	go, no, so	find, kind
Reading Long Words	✓ start	✓	✓	✓	✓	✓	✓	✓	✓	✓
Magic -e-	✓	✓	✓							
Word Endings					Review		Review			
Pair Practice	✓ nonwords									
Book Reading	Willy's Wish Bob Books B-2	Funny Bunny Bob Books B-1			Jumper and the Clown Bob Books B-2			Samantha Bob Books B-2		

*Only newly introduced words listed.

Lesson Component Scope and Sequence

COMPONENTS	71	72	73	74	75	76	77	78	79	80
					LESSONS					
New Letter Sounds/Pairs	Review	ir	Review	Review	kn-	wr-	Review	-ng	Review	-nk
Say the Sounds (and Write Sounds)	ai, ay, ea, ee, oa, oo, ou	ay, ea, ee, [ir], oa, oo, ou, ow	ai, ea, ee, er, ir, oo, ou, ow, ue	ai, al, ar, ay, ch, ea, ee, er, ew, ir, oa, oo, qu, sh, ue, wh	knife, knee, kneel, knelt, knight, knit, knob, knock, knot	wrap, wreath, wrench, wrist, write, wrote	knead, knitting, knotted, wreck, wring	banging, bring, clanging, ding, fangs, gang, hanging, long, lungs, ring, sing, song, swing, stringy, things	hanger, long, ringing, sang, strong, stung, swing, wings	honk, ink, junk, mink, pink, stink, tanker, sinking, yanked
Word Reading (and Spelling)*	beater, cheat, deep, healing, meets, nailing, reads, street, treats, wheat	birch, birth, boats, dirt, fir, first, flight, girls, owls, peach, peek, sir, steaming, stir	birds, growl, shampoo, shirt, sneak, squirm, thirsty, whirl	booklet, choke, coaster, hunter, march, mighty, shine, skirt, toad, trash, walrus, while	beast, crook, doorknob, kicked, knead, knits, knotty, marsh, penknife, saint, scarf, stout	chart, chirps, east, knapsack, kneecap, rooster, shark, shipwreck, started, twisted, unwrap, waist, write	croak, kneepad, knock, smirk, snail, swirl, third, wrong	brightly, chained, fainted, freeway, mouth, reaching, showers, slang, slingshot, slouching, string, sung, twirl	brings, clanging, daylight, falling, gaining, trailing, loudest, pleated, reached, rounded, slightly	blink, charcoal, coach, hunk, shrunk, Spain, spool, springs, squirt, staying, stinking, tattoo, thanks, trunk
Sight Words	both	where	Review	Review	Review	talk, walk	Review	because	put	four, your
Reading Long Words	✓									
Double Consonants		✓ starts	✓	✓						
Book Reading	*The Class Trip* Scholastic Books		*The Game* Bob Books C-1		*The Big Red Sled* Scholastic Books		*Joe's Toe* Bob Books C-1		*The Picnic* Bob Books C-1	

*Only newly introduced words listed.

Lesson Component Scope and Sequence

Sound Partners

LESSONS

COMPONENTS	81	82	83	84	85	86	87	88	89	90
New Letter Sounds/ Pairs	Review	c /s/	g /j/	Review	Review	or	Review	aw	Review	Review
Say the Sounds (and Write Sounds)	blink, bonk, plank, spring, think, wrapper	cell, cellar, cent, center, cinder, circus, face, fancy, ice, Pacific, pencil, place	age, energy, gelatin, gem, gently, germ, ginger, gym, huge, large, page, rage	lace, rice	central, Cindy, price, spice	border, cork, for, forbid, forest, morning, normal, orbit, order, pork, sorts, sport	boring, corner, dormitory, florist, glory, horn, hornet, ordering, stork, shorter	awful, awkward, claw, crawl, gawk, lawn, outlaw, paws, raw, seesaw, shawl, straw	brawny, dawn, hawk, paws, saw, sawmill, yawning	cigar, skunk, thorn
Word Reading (and Spelling)*	chirps, clank, clink, headstrong, meantime, nightmare, sour, stream	acid, bringing, crosswalk, flashlight, honk, ice cream, knickers, off-side, painting, pencil, pound-ing, quicker, rocket, sticking, stinger	banker, check-book, energy, face, gerbil, nightgown, playground, rocks, slice, stage, staff, stiffer	ace, bumper, fence	canter, mice, pigpen, slicker, whirling	corn, foghorn, forty, hang, hornpipe, lucky, popcorn, shock, shortest, sort-ing, steaming, stem, sticker, stork, story	bricks, corn-husk, forks, seaport, short-hand, shouting, snoring, streaky, strike	cheating, check-ers, crawling, flick-ers, glide, glory, jaws, jawbone, jigsaw, meaty, playing, sprayer, wheat	awful, jaywalk, mainstream, north, organ, plywood, port, short, Sunday, torn, yucky	banker, drain, gently, knock-out, pocket, shipwreck, stuffy, thawing, written
Sight Words*	Review	do	move	Review	friend	sure	little	shiny	again	Review
Reading Long Words									✓	✓
Book Reading	*The Picnic* Bob Books C-1		*Bed Bugs* Bob Books B-1		*The King, Part I* Bob Books C-1		*The King, Part II* Bob Books C-1		*The Train* Bob Books C-1	

*Only newly introduced words listed.

Lesson Component Scope and Sequence

COMPONENTS	91	92	93	94	95	96	97	98	99	100
					LESSONS					
New Letter Sounds/ Pairs	-le	be-, de-, pre-, re-	-tion, -sion	Review	ur	Review	Review	ey	Review	oi, oy
Say the Sounds (and Write Sounds)	angle, ankle, buckle, circle, dribble, gentle, simple, shuffle, tickle	begin, belong, defend, detect, pretend, prevent, repay, retell, return	action, direction, election, fraction, friction, mansion, mission, section, subtraction, suction, tension, vision	betray, decision, detach, knuckle, mention, retire	burn, burst, church, disturb, fur, hurt, purr, surf, turn	blurry, burp, churn, nurse, turning	aw, be-, de-, ir, kn, -le, -ng, -nk, or, pre-, re-, -sion, -tion, ur, wr	alley, donkey, hockey, honey, key, kidney, money, turkey, valley		boil, coins, enjoy, joins, joy, moist, noisy, pointed, royal, soil, soy, spoiling, toys, voice
Word Reading (and Spelling)*	corks, cricket, crinkle, dimple, fangs, feast, jacket, little, pluck, singer, stork, stumble, thimble, thorny	began, below, beside, between, border, decay, delight, detach, gently, portray, predict, reply, request, remote, settle	babble, buckle, chuckle, demand, direction, fly, helicopter, junction, relate, session, traction	attention, behave, crumble, decide, portion, precise, recess, scribble, sniffle, stubble, trickle	action, blurry, crawl, drifted, helps, horn, hurt, portion, simple, smelling, swelled, torch, yelled	further, hurry, invention, nursery, purple, shelter, smelly, turnips, turtle	depend, gurgle, knuckle, mention, reduction, reorder, throttle, wrinkle	barley, corndog, decoration, drove, nursing, spelling, spurs, sweltering	birdcage, burner, construction, demanding, furnish, hurdle, infection, monkey, northerner, reporting, sawmill, slurp	boiler, cowboy, dirty, foil, joint, jungle, oily, oyster, pointed, spoiled, soybean, twinkle
Sight Words	brother, mother, other	could, couldn't, should, shouldn't, would, wouldn't	busy	bought, thought	tiny	Review	Review	cried, toward	paper, sorry	beautiful, laugh
Contraction Review						✓ starts				
Reading Long Words	✓	✓	✓	✓	✓	✓	✓	✓	✓	✓
Book Reading	*The Train* Bob Books C-1	*Chickens* Bob Books C-1			*The Visit* Bob Books C-1		Review	*Shipwreck Saturday* Chapter 1 Scholastic Books	*Shipwreck Saturday* Chapter 2 Scholastic Books	*Shipwreck Saturday* Chapter 3 Scholastic Books

*Only newly introduced words listed.

Lesson Component Scope and Sequence

Sound Partners

COMPONENTS	LESSONS 101	102	103	104	105	106	107	108
New Letter Sounds/Pairs	Review	Review	ow /ō/	Review	ph	Review	Cumulative Review	Cumulative Review
Say the Sounds (and Write Sounds)	broil, destroy, doily, moist, Roy	awnings, decoy, spoiled, tinfoil	blow, borrow, bowl, bowling, bowtie, flow, follow, growing, know, lower, mower, owner, snowball, tow, window, yellow	glowing, slowest, snowstorm, throwing, towboat	alphabet, dolphin, elephant, nephew, phantom, phone, photo, phrase, telegraph	graph, orphan, phase, photo, trophy, typhoon	aw, be-, de-, ey, kn, -le, oi, or, ow, oy, ph, pre-, -tion, ur, wr	er, ey, -le, kn, oi, or, ow, oy, ph, pre-, pre-, -sion, -tion, ur, wr
Word Reading (and Spelling)*	employ, enjoy, invention, jiggle, saddle	attention, corduroy, corner, crumble, embroider, employment, loyal, keychain, prevention, royalty, Thursday, yawning	lawnmower, owner, prediction, pursue, sorted, towboat, wiggles, willow	bundle, clawing, informed, inspection, joyful, snowplow, sprinkle, stripe	avenue, clues, coasters, handle, Memphis, noodle, phew, Phil, partners, statue, stowaway, telephone, thousands, Troy	enjoyment, marching, moody, photograph, railroad, starving, tissue, Tuesday	bottle, elbow, expression, lighter, reflection, spine	blade, knight, ointment, rattle, remark, snuggle, tighten
Sight Words	neighbor, through	cookies, eight	enough, lion	cherry, eggs	piece, strange	cold, hold		
Reading Long Words	✓	✓	✓	✓	✓	✓	✓	✓
Book Reading	Poppleton and Friends Chapter 1 Scholastic Books	Poppleton and Friends Chapter 2 Scholastic Books	Poppleton and Friends Chapter 3 Scholastic Books	Poppleton Forever Chapter 1 Scholastic Books	Poppleton Forever Chapter 2 Scholastic Books	Poppleton Forever Chapter 3 Scholastic Books	Reread favorite stories!	Reread favorite stories!

*Only newly introduced words listed.

Sound Partners

Mastery Test Directions for Administration and Scoring

Administer each Mastery Test soon after the student has completed every tenth lesson. Use the Mastery Test to check that the student has learned the skills taught in those lessons and to gauge how much review to provide. The Mastery Tests are best administered by someone other than the student's regular tutor, although we know this can be difficult to arrange.

The Mastery Tests can also be used by the program supervisor to place a student who needs to start further along in the lessons. Find the Mastery Test on which the student scores less than 90% (e.g., Mastery Test 4, Lessons 31–40) and begin instruction at that point in the lessons (i.e., start at Lesson 31).

Materials

- ► Tester copy of Mastery Test
- ► Student copy of Mastery Test
- ► Student Recording Sheet
- ► Pencils for student and tester

Administration

1. Place student copy of Mastery Test in front of student.

2. Place your copy of Mastery Test in a position so that the student cannot see what you read or record.

3. Say the directions provided for each part of the test on the tester copy. There are three test parts: Sounds (saying the sounds and writing the sounds), Word Reading/Sight Word Reading, and Spelling.

4. Mark incorrect student responses with a slash.

5. Add the total correct responses for each part. (Add the responses for both saying sounds and writing sounds for the Sounds total.)

6. For Sounds writing and Spelling words, have the student use the Student Recording Sheet.

7. At the end of testing, review the student's scores. For any section on which the test indicates more review, incorporate this review into your regular instruction.

Scoring

1. If the student cannot identify a letter sound or read a word within three seconds, score the item incorrect and move to the next item. Say, "Let's try the next one."

2. If the student makes an error and then corrects the error within three seconds, score the item as correct.

3. Remind the student to write clearly so that you can distinguish correct spelling.

4. Do not penalize the student for imprecise pronunciation due to dialect, articulation, or second-language issues. Use your knowledge of how the student usually pronounces sounds to decide whether the student is producing his or her closest approximation to the correct sound.

Suggestions

1. If you (the tutor) are using the Mastery Test to monitor student progress, and your student scores below 70%, talk to your supervisor. Review whether you are implementing the lessons correctly, and have your supervisor observe and provide suggestions.

2. Keep a file of each student's Mastery Tests so that you can refer to these tests to monitor student progress over time. Share the tests with the classroom teacher for use in instructional decision-making.

Initial Tutor Training Checklist

Supervisor: _____ Date: _____

Tutor: _____

Observe tutors practicing instruction during their initial training. These are the basic tutor behaviors that trainers should see each tutor demonstrate. Trainers can use the form to give tutors feedback on their practice.

Component	Criteria	Yes	No
Say the Sounds	1. Models sounds in box correctly.		
	2. Coaches student to say sounds from left to right while fingerpointing.		
	3. Follows lesson sequence/script.		
Segmenting	1. Says word (requires student to listen, not read).		
	2. Points to each box when segmenting (student and tutor).		
	3. Models correctly (says word, segments sounds into boxes, and says word).		
	4. Follows lesson sequence/script.		
Word Reading	1. Models sounding out without stopping between sounds (word in box).		
	2. Selects spelling words with varying beginning, middle, and ending sounds.		
	3. Follows lesson sequence/script.		
Sight Words	1. Models new word (says, spells, and says word).		
	2. Follows lesson sequence/script.		
Sentence Reading	1. Requires student to fingerpoint.		
	2. Uses appropriate error-correction procedure (isolates difficult sound, supplies word, rereads sentence).		
	3. Follows lesson sequence/script.		
Magic -e- (Begins Lesson 46)	1. Demonstrates each step of using the rule.		
	2. Follows lesson sequence/script.		
Word Endings (Begins Lesson 21)	1. Models by pointing and saying the word ending with a word.		
	2. Corrects by reminding student of word ending.		
	3. Follows lesson sequence/script.		
Pair Practice (Begins Lesson 43)	1. Says letter pairs (by using sounds, not letter names) for student to spell.		
	2. Follows lesson sequence/script.		
Reading Long Words (Begins Lesson 61)	1. Has student break word into parts, then read whole word.		
	2. Corrects by isolating each part for student, then has student read each part and whole word.		
	3. Follows lesson sequence/script.		
Book Reading (Begins Lesson 6)	1. Demonstrates reading methods (independent, partner, and echo).		
	2. Models fingerpointing and rereading.		
	3. Shows two error-correction procedures (isolates difficult sound, supplies word/repeats).		
	4. Identifies correct reading steps (new book twice, last book once, previously read books).		
Overall Tutor Instruction	1. Models lesson components correctly.		
	2. Is receptive to corrective feedback.		
	3. Demonstrates appropriate correction strategy.		
	4. Provides examples of specific praise.		
	5. Demonstrates levels of scaffolding (e.g., more coaching, added practice).		
Strengths			
Improvement Suggestions			

Follow-up Tutor Training
Proficiency Checklist

Supervisor: _____ Date: _____

Tutor: _____

Use this checklist to observe tutors after they have had one to two weeks to use the lessons with their students and to give the tutors additional coaching. This checklist includes the critical tutor behaviors as well as correction and scaffolding.

Component	Criteria	Yes	No
Say the Sounds	1. Models correct sounds [error sounds _____].		
	2. Detects and provides extra practice on weak sounds (by reviewing at the end).		
	3. Says the sounds for the student to write (new sounds, difficult sounds, and one easy sound).		
	4. Provides an example of specific praise for this component.		
	5. Follows lesson sequence/script.		
Segmenting	1. Says word (requires student to listen, not read; covers words).		
	2. Has student point to each box when segmenting (says word, segments, and says word).		
	3. Models correctly (says word, segments sounds into boxes, and says word).		
	4. Provides an example of specific praise for this component.		
	5. Follows lesson sequence/script.		
Word Reading	1. Models sounding out without stopping between sounds (word in box).		
	2. Has student sound out words without stopping between sounds.		
	3. Directs student to difficult sound in word (helps student blend together).		
	4. Has student spell three words, including new and difficult words (says, spells, and reads).		
	5. Provides added practice for difficult words.		
	6. Provides an example of specific praise for this component.		
	7. Follows lesson sequence/script.		
All Spelling Tasks	1. Requires student to segment sounds in words.		
	2. Has student read all written words.		
	3. Provides added practice for difficult words.		
	4. Provides an example of specific praise for this component.		
	5. Follows lesson sequence/script.		
Sight Words	1. Models new word in box.		
	2. Requires student to read, spell aloud, and then reread words (while fingerpointing).		
	3. Provides added practice on difficult words (reads, spells aloud, and rereads).		
	4. Provides an example of specific praise for this component.		
	5. Follows lesson sequence/script.		
All Sentence & Text Reading Tasks	1. Requires student to fingerpoint to each word while reading.		
	2. Requires student to reread any sentence with an error (added practice).		
	3. Requires student to use sounding out when needed.		
	4. Corrects by directing student to the difficult part of the word.		
	5. Provides an example of specific praise for this component.		
	6. Follows lesson sequence/script.		
Magic -e- (Begins Lesson 46)	1. Uses script to provide practice on each step of using the rule.		
	2. Corrects by reminding student of the rule (letter positions).		
	3. Provides an example of specific praise for this component.		
	4. Follows lesson sequence/script.		

Follow-up Tutor Training
Proficiency Checklist

Supervisor: _____ Date: _____

Tutor: _____

Use this checklist to observe tutors after they have had one to two weeks to use the lessons with their students and to give the tutors additional coaching. This checklist includes the critical tutor behaviors as well as correction and scaffolding.

Component	Criteria	Yes	No
Word Endings (Begins Lesson 21)	1. Models by pointing and saying the word ending *with a word* (not in isolation).		
	2. Has student say words with ending.		
	3. Corrects by reminding student of word ending.		
	4. Provides an example of specific praise for this component.		
	5. Follows lesson sequence/script.		
Magic -e- (Begins Lesson 46)	1. Uses script to provide practice on each step of using the rule.		
	2. Corrects by reminding student of the rule (letter positions).		
	3. Provides an example of specific praise for this component.		
	4. Follows lesson sequence/script.		
Pair Practice (Begins Lesson 43)	1. Dictates the letter pairs (by using sounds, not letter names) for student to spell.		
	2. Has student read all words, spell, and reread words.		
	3. Corrects by drawing attention to the difficult letter-pair and having student reread.		
	4. Follows lesson sequence/script.		
Reading Long Words (Begins Lesson 61)	1. Has student break word into parts, then read whole word.		
	2. Corrects by isolating each part for student, then has student read each part and whole word.		
	3. Follows lesson sequence/script.		
Book Reading (Begins Lesson 6)	1. Follows correct reading steps (new book twice, last book once, and previously read books).		
	2. Demonstrates three methods of reading (independent, partner, and echo).		
	3. Uses standard error-correction procedures (isolates difficulty, supplies/repeats, and chunks parts).		
	4. Follows lesson sequence/script (e.g., correct book selection).		
Overall Tutor Instruction	1. Models lesson components correctly.		
	2. Corrects all errors immediately.		
	3. Corrects student without negative comments.		
	4. Provides examples of specific praise.		
	5. Demonstrates efficient pacing.		
	6. Isolates difficult sounds.		
	7. Demonstrates levels of scaffolding (e.g., more coaching, added practice).		
Strengths			
Improvement Suggestions			